GYRA Golf

GYRA Golf

Golf's 1st Mental Scorecard

Dr. Izzy Justice

GYRA GOLF
Golf's 1st Mental Scorecard

iUniverse books may be ordered through booksellers or by contacting:

iUniverse
1663 Liberty Drive
Bloomington, IN 47403
www.iuniverse.com
1-800-Authors (1-800-288-4677)

Because of the dynamic nature of the Internet, any web addresses or links contained in this book may have changed since publication and may no longer be valid. The views expressed in this work are solely those of the author and do not necessarily reflect the views of the publisher, and the publisher hereby disclaims any responsibility for them.

Any people depicted in stock imagery provided by Getty Images are models, and such images are being used for illustrative purposes only. Certain stock imagery © Getty Images.

ISBN: 978-1-6632-0058-7 (sc)
ISBN: 978-1-6632-0057-0 (e)

Library of Congress Control Number: 2020909443

Print information available on the last page.

iUniverse rev. date: 06/08/2020

Dedication

To Stephanie, Lexi, Hunter, and my eternal mentor, Gary Mason.

Acknowledgments

This book would not be possible without the input of so many golfers who participated in the invaluable research and insight into this book. Special thanks to Gary Player, Hunter Justice, David Ross, Matt Ryan, Tim Straub, Seamus Power, Jason Gore, Courtney Hall, Cornel Driessen, and my editor, Anjum Khan.

Contents

Foreword

I love how golf can bring people, friends, families, and communities together – as I've always said, golf is a friendship factory! It is a gift of time. When I design courses, I take pride in knowing thousands of conversations are going to occur on the property. Memories will be made. Golfers will have a chance to beat their best every time they play. I love knowing that, as a designer and architect of holes, I am testing not just the physical ability of the golfer, but also the ability to make decisions, take risk-reward challenges, take pride in conquering the course, and view failures as a challenge to come back and give it another go. I know I am testing the human brain and its capacity to make good and poor decisions, to create narratives, good and bad, and to tell stories of the battle that occurred on the golf course. I know this because I did the same as a player. I know that I enjoyed the test and I loved the memories of the challenges. I know that the test is both physical and mental, and frankly, more mental than physical.

So you can imagine my surprise when the concept of a "mental scorecard" was introduced to me. I was quite intrigued as I had not heard of such a thing. Keep a mental score after each shot and each hole? What? How? I know we keep score after each hole, number of shots taken, and this is a measure of your battle against the course. Every golfer knows that the first battle on the course is not against the course, it is against oneself. Can we recover from a bad shot? Can we recover from a bad break? Did we consider all the factors correctly before picking the club and choosing the shot to hit? Is there a way to measure this mental battle?

If you can describe your shoes or any golf club better than you can describe your brain, then you are like the rest of us. This world of neuroscience, understanding how the brain works, has always intrigued me. Technology is allowing us to go inside the tiny neurons of the brain and see where they are going when over a critical putt, after a bad shot, or hole or bad break, and understand for the first time what is happening.

The notion that we can "keep mental score" was completely foreign to me until I read Dr. Justice's work. What a game-changing concept! Why not keep mental score when keeping golf score on the same scorecard? Why not use the mental scores to make adjustments? The golfer's brain is constantly working, negotiating with itself, playing roles of judge, jury, prosecutor, defendant, and narrator of the past and future, all without our understanding of what is really happening. Win the mental score first and then you can take on the golf course. This is the right order of battle. I know this to be true from my own experience. The most frustrating part about golf is not losing, but when you lose because of your own mental or emotional mistakes, when you perform below what you know you are capable of.

Dr. Izzy Justice has created golf's first mental scorecard. Unbelievable! It is simple; it is kept on the same scorecard as the golf score, no devices needed, so that you know exactly where your brain is after each shot. This book is easy to read and understand so that you can get to know your own brain as well as any of your clubs. I can see how any golfer of any level would find great value in this. You may never play golf the same way if you start measuring your mental performance on the golf course.

Gary Player
World Golf Hall of Fame
Nine-Time Major Winner
165 Professional Victories over five decades

Introduction

I am proud to share the first golf mental scorecard that is based on the results of a 12-month longitudinal, neuroscience-based research study on the correlation of emotional state, brain activity, and quality of golf shots. Golfers from all levels were taught an easy-to-understand model, GYRA, and asked to keep their emotional and mental score per shot and per hole on the same traditional golf scorecard. The randomized data from 500 of these scorecards was entered into a database that allowed us to draw conclusions on the impact of poor shots on subsequent shots. Certain shots correlated to half-stroke cost while others were a full-stroke cost to the overall score. I will lay out the neuroscience used, explain the GYRA model, share how costs are calculated, describe tools to use to adjust for these costs, and end with a first-hand account from a professional on how to use this model to essentially make you your own sports psychologist when you are playing so you can make better decisions and perform to your potential. To learn more, go to www.gyragolf.com.

As a sports neuropsychologist, I have worked with professional athletes, coaches, and teams in many sports, as well as with business professionals for three decades specializing in Emotional Intelligence (EQ). When working with golfers and golf instructors, I always start by asking them to describe their driver to me. Invariably, it is usually quite detailed. Most can tell me their brand, length of shaft, stiffness, flex points, club head size, loft, grip type and size, and so on. I then ask them to describe their brain. You can visualize the blank stare response. Golfers use a driver about 14 times a round. They use their brain on every shot, between shots, before a round, and after a round. It is the brain that creates the running commentary, where decisions are made on club/shot selection and course management, and where the signal is created and transported to the muscles to execute those decisions. I have found a profound deficiency in golfers in their understanding of the brain. Equally deficient is emotional literacy to label and adjust the spectrum of emotions felt through the course of a round. This book will provide that brain understanding and emotional literacy so that as a golfer, the 'club' you use on every shot, your brain, is as familiar to you as your driver.

It should be noted that this book is not a golf instruction book. I do not teach you how to swing any club. There is no substitute for being taught how to swing any golf club, or for a player understanding the mechanics behind a poor shot; and for that, I wish to acknowledge the invaluable role of golf teaching professionals. However, if you know how to hit a particular shot — and you have done it many times before successfully at your command — but that skill is not showing up in a critical situation, that is where this book comes in. If you find yourself saying, "I am underperforming!" or, "Where did that come from?" or, "I can't believe I just did that!" or, "I don't know why I did that," then this book will answer those questions. When my phone rings, it is not because of any score that a player has just shot, it is because the player does not understand why he or she underperformed.

Golf Background

Golf is played in more than 200 countries. There are over 34,000 golf courses in the world. The U.S. has the most, with over 15,000. In 2005, player participation in the U.S. was at its peak, with roughly 30 million players. Shortly after that, numbers dropped steeply to around 24 million. In the last four years, the numbers have increased and are holding steady at around 25 million players.

There are 1,289 men's college golf programs and 939 women's programs. Division One programs have the highest number of teams from both sexes, with 299 men's and 262 women's programs. For these Division One programs, over $9 million are given out in scholarships combined.

The top five world golf markets are: (i) U.S., (ii) Japan, (iii) South Korea, (iv) U.K., and (v) Canada. These five markets represent 80%

of total equipment sales. The U.S. and Japan control over 65% of the world market. In 2015, golf generated $8.7 billion globally.

The two governing bodies are the United States Golf Association (USGA) and the R&A. The USGA was founded in 1894 and is the governing body in the U.S. and Mexico only. The R&A was originally founded in 1754 as the *Society of St. Andrews Golfers* (in Scotland), and it governs the rest of the world.

One can discern from all these hard statistics that golf is a lucrative and global sport, and growing at the junior levels at an unprecedented rate. What these facts do not show is the spirit and soul of golf.

Golf is as much a sport as it is a social and business enterprise. There are vast housing developments built around golf courses so that homes can have views of fairways, greens, flowers and ponds. There are social events, such as Member-Guest tournaments, that usually are the annual highlight for most clubs. Golfers take golf trips around the country and world to build friendships and take a break from the hustle and bustle of work and family life. Vacations are planned around golf destinations that also cater to non-golfers with amenities like spas.

A ton of business is also conducted on the golf course. Corporate outings and business dealings are a norm as the change in scenery from office space is often welcome, not to mention an emotionally-disarming environment.

There is also the relaxation and physical health component that most retirees cherish. It feels great to get out of the house, and go out with little physical stress and walk on fairways. Many find it therapeutic as the social interaction with friends in an outdoor setting just feels good.

Golf as an Endurance Sport

It can be easy to forget, given all these benefits of the game of golf, that it is a sport requiring skills that has measurable outcomes. Golf, for all practical purposes, is an endurance sport. An average round of golf for 18 holes lasts about 4.5 hours. That is about the same time it takes on average to complete a full marathon of 26.2 miles, or just an hour less than a half Ironman event of 1.2 miles of swimming, 56 miles of riding a bike, and 13.1 miles of running.

What makes golf the ultimate endurance test is that it is quite literally 93% mental and 7% physical. How so? It takes anywhere between 5 and 15 seconds to actually hit a golf shot; that is, to draw a club back and strike the ball physically. With an average score of 85 shots for 18 holes, that is less than 20 minutes of physical activity. This means that for a 4.5-hour round, 4.1 hours are spent on non-physical activity that very few golfers have any plan for. **It begs the question of why almost 100% of time training for golf is spent on the physical activity, yet almost no time is spent on effectively managing the large amount of time between shots?**

I speak at events about 20-30 times a year and often ask golfers: What percentage of golf is mental versus physical? The lowest mental number I have heard is 60% and the highest is 95%. I have found that the better the golfer, the higher the percentage of the mental side is acknowledged. **It begs another question of why, if both the quantitative time and the actual percentage of skill (60-95%) required is mental, there is almost no time spent training for this?**

This book is largely about managing that 93% of time so that when you are ready to hit a shot, your emotions and thoughts are in the best place possible for the shot to come out as you want. It is about recognizing that, just because you are not hitting a shot 93% of the time, the brain is still working, processing past and future shots. If the brain is left to do what it naturally does, that is a wasted opportunity. It is about having a plan to play golf to give you the best chance of being fully ready (mentally, emotionally, and physically) to hit the next shot to the best of your ability, whatever that ability is.

The central premise of this book is that golf is as much an emotional and mental endurance test as it is a golf skill test.

In trying to understand why little to no time is spent training for the emotional and mental test of golf, of the many reasons offered and researched, I have found one cause more compelling than all others. As a tour pro confessed, "I don't even know exactly what I'm supposed to do to mentally prepare or grow." This is because there is no measurement of the mental side of golf.

In all sports, and golf is no different in this regard, the measurements of the physical side of the sport are abundant. In basketball, stats are provided for the number of minutes played, shots taken, shots made, rebounds, assists, and 3-points made. In golf, just go to the PGA Tour website, pick any pro, and under their profile you will find more statistics than you are likely to understand. The most common ones are score, fairways hit, greens hit, and putts made. For tour players, there are about 20 other measurements available. Because of these measurable results, it is easy to identify areas of improvement. If you only hit 2 fairways in your round, then you likely need to work on your driver. If you took 54 putts, 3 per hole, then you likely need to work on your putting. Measurements allow us to identify areas of strength and weakness, thus making it logical to know what to work on to improve.

However, as noted in the earlier paragraphs, the consensus is largely that golf is driven not by these measurable physical skills, but actually by the mental ones. In Chapter 2, I will show neurologically that, in fact, the physical golf skill rests on first the emotional and mental state of the brain. In other words, those golf statistics we measure are more dependent on other variables (emotional and mental) than on the proficiency of golf skills themselves.

What if there was a mental scorecard that allowed you to do the same things as the other golf metrics? What if the mental score per hole, and even per shot, allowed you to know exactly where you are emotionally and mentally? Could the metrics help you make adjustments while you are playing? Once the round is complete, could the mental scorecard be used to identify what to work on, to improve? Could a mental scorecard provide an answer to the tour pro's question of knowing what to actually do to build mental strength? The answer is YES!

The emotional and mental endurance test that is golf requires a scorecard that can identify the true root cause of poor shots.

It is worth repeating the question many good golfers ask me: "I don't even know what to work on so I can be mentally stronger when I'm playing?" If your putting is off, you have dozens of drills and training aids to help. If your bunker play is off, and the statistics show your bunker save-percentage is low, then you know to get a lesson on bunker play and work on it. If your swing is off, you may have an instructor who knows your swing and knows what is off. But in the hours of practice time you have, what exactly are you supposed to be doing to grow mentally?

This book presents what I believe to be the first Golf Mental Scorecard, called the GYRA Scorecard. I will share how to train your brain off the golf course to become mentally stronger during practice time; and how to use the score card when playing to properly identify the root cause of a bad shot (or hole or sequence of shots/holes) so that the adjustments can be made and rounds/scores can be saved.

"Crises are part of life. Everybody has to face them, and it doesn't make any difference what the crisis is." -Jack Nicklaus

I will also introduce you to a sequence of emotional and mental preparation, before, during, and after a round, as well as for practice. You will be introduced to a new emotional and mental language similar to the physical language of golf. In the latter, golfers know what a bunker is, what fairways, greens or rough are, and what a putter is versus an iron or a driver or wedge. We know what a fade, draw, hook, and slice are.

These are all words that form a language that allow you to understand the physical game of golf. Yet, we do not even have a language to understand our own brain or emotions; words that we can use in the same way to properly label and adjust what is going on during the round.

In addition to a new language, you will build your own personal game plan. No two human beings are the same emotionally and mentally, so the plan for each person will be different and has to accommodate the emotional fluctuations of both life and golf, where highs and lows can impact so much of decision-making. I call this the **"software"** of each person, as opposed to the hardware, which is our physical and biological bodies, which are virtually identical in function. Your software is different from any other human in the world, even though you have the same organs and body parts as everyone in the world.

During a round of golf, the sheer volume of monologues (software) that occur is quite unprecedented. Each monologue, that self-talk and commentary, after almost every shot, is a natural human response to the stimuli of the ever-changing environment. Whether it is the tee box, the wind, the rain, the heat, the playing partner, the lie, the pin position, the inconsistent greens, bunkers, or fairways, or whatever myriad of unique circumstances that literally each shot presents, the environment in golf is constantly changing and challenging. Compound this with the competitive environment of whoever you are playing with or against, your expectations or handicap, no teammates or coaches to help you, as well as the countless things that can go wrong, we are talking about a brain that has an enormous amount of activity to process. Your software is working non-stop and largely without any proactive conscious direction from you. It is just doing its thing. **The brain activity when playing competitively is not the same brain activity when playing casually, not even close.** In effect, the brain used on the driving range, practice area, practice rounds, casual rounds, is not the same brain as when you play competitively, thereby making the overwhelming majority of range and practice time quite ineffective. Would you go to the first tee with a set of clubs that you have not used in a while? No. This is what you are doing by not training the brain for the actual mental conditions of competition. It is why many say the hardest shot in golf is the first one off the first tee because it *feels* different.

These emotions and thoughts, both good and not so good ones, will dictate the tone and content of the monologues and critical subsequent decision-making throughout the round. In Chapter 1, I will share several stories that almost all golfers will be able to relate to; where they themselves got in their own way, failed to execute their strategy for the physical game, and underperformed.

Yet, despite powerful personal stories of underperformance and many more well-documented ones from professional golfers, the average golfer still spends almost zero time training his or her emotions and thoughts. I researched dozens of golf training programs and videos and found very few that had budgeted time for this kind of training.

When asked what is the most difficult shot in golf, the most common answers I get are the first tee shot or a 40-yard bunker shot, or a few will say the next shot. **It is my absolute contention that the most difficult shot in golf is the one right after a bad one**. Why? As I will explain in Chapter 2, right after a bad shot, the emotional temperature is so high that cognitive decision-making is neurologically compromised, leading to a very low probability that you can either make the right next decision or physically execute that next shot to the best of your ability. What shows up as a "bad shot" was actually caused by the brain processing the previous shot, unable to *focus* on the shot at hand. Golfers have had no way to measure the emotional/mental cost of that previous bad shot. Not all bad shots have the same cost. Missing a two-foot putt for birdie is not the same as missing a two-foot putt for bogey. Even though both are equal in stroke count, they are not emotionally/mentally equal. Both are costly, but the latter is much more expensive. Making a double bogey *feels* much worse than making par in terms of cost. **The GYRA Scorecard creates an Emotional and Mental Accounting System that**

allows you to assess the correct neurological cost, and then make the right adjustment to redirect the brain so that the cost is never high enough to impact the next shot.

"It's easy to hit a great shot when feeling good, it's really tough to hit a good shot when feeling bad." -Bob Torrance

This is the reason to write this book: to allow golfers to measure each shot and each hole with a score that can best reflect the mental cost and state, so that they can go to the next shot and execute it to their best.

This book is not about swinging the golf club correctly, putting correctly, getting more distance or the short game, nor is it about any equipment. There are plenty of resources for these dimensions of the sport that are readily available. Golfers are notorious for buying anything that they believe will make them perform better, but there is no off-the-shelf equipment for rewriting your software to manage your thoughts and emotions. **This is a personal endeavor.**

"Every man dies. Not every man really lives." -William Wallace

This book brings decades of experience and neuroscience working with elite athletes, coaches, golfers, and amateurs. I hope this book will be an invaluable asset to your practice and round of golf. I will start the book with real-life stories to prove that golf is indeed an emotional and mental test, more so than physical. Then, I will provide you with detailed and easily understandable neuroscience of how the human body works: what emotions and thoughts are and how they are created; and how to recognize, label, and manage them during practice, pre-tournament anxieties, and each situation in your round. The chapters will build GYRA tools, 14 of them, like a set of clubs, to use to make adjustments. Finally, a tour player will take you through a full week of how the GYRA scorecard and tools were used in a pressure environment like Q School.

You will learn not just mental tips to be a better golfer, but also understand *why* that tip will work for *you* from a neuroscience perspective. The explicit intention is that you fully understand why these tips work so you can make adjustments as warranted, instead of just doing random things and hoping they work. This combination of knowledge is guaranteed to help you with your goals, and almost surely, with your personal journey of growth as well. It will answer the question, "What can I do to grow mentally?"

The goal of this book is that you will use the GYRA Scorecard, conveniently identical to the traditional scorecard of any golf course, in all your rounds to help you win the first challenge of the test of golf – your emotional and mental state. Winning this will allow you to showcase your golf skills when it counts the most.

Essentially, two books are being provided to you – one that I wrote, and the other written by you in the spaces provided in this book because your software is unique to you and only you. **Thus, if you do all of the written exercises suggested, you will have a second book written by you, and for you. Either or both of these books can be read many times over during your season.** Your book will provide you the necessary emotional/mental "clubs" to use per situation that are unique to you so that you can use them while using the GYRA Scorecard.

Emotional endurance and mental strength are not just a part of golf, but also a part of life. It can be argued that life itself is an emotional endurance test. And this may be what makes golf so popular, as you can draw parallels between training for and playing a round, and your own life's journey. It is possible to feel many highs and lows and everything in between in a round of golf – a microcosm of life. I hope that the reader-interactive format will impact both your physical and emotional endurance to help you perform to the best of your ability when it counts the most.

Chapter 1

- *The question is never, "What do I feel?" It is, "What memory of mine is being associated with this experience?"*
- *Neurologically speaking, life can be effectively described as a series of biased interpretations of experience. As awful as this sounds, it does suggest that if interpretation itself can be altered, and not experiences, life can be quite different.*
- *I often ask a trick question to athletes: What do you do if you want to get to really know someone? I always get good responses. I then ask: How many of those things do you do to get to know yourself? In the middle of competition is not the right time to learn about yourself!*

@izzyjustice

Why Train in EQ?

So why invest in learning about the brain and Emotional Intelligence (EQ)? I recognize that you are already spending hours on the range, on the putting green, in the short game area playing with 14 different clubs, each of which you can use to hit a variety of shots depending on grip, swing, force of strike, and so on. There is a lot to practice in the physical game of golf and shots to have. There are also all the equipment changes that come out every year from clubs to grips, balls, and so much more.

So why add yet one more dimension to your practice plan? Perhaps the best way to establish the case for this is to review several examples of what happens all the time in golf and other sports. Below are actual stories by professionals and amateurs alike. I had literally hundreds to choose from, but selected just a few that underscore the fact that mis-hits (bad shots) are virtually guaranteed to occur in golf, and it is your emotional response to them that can be the difference between underperforming and recovering to overachieve.

"I think maybe I hit only one perfect shot a round." –Jack Nicklaus

➢ In the 1989 Masters, Scott Hoch had a one-shot lead with two holes to go. As he walked to the 17th tee, he said he started thinking about winning the tournament for the first time. He hit his drive into the 15th fairway, from where he said he made a mental mistake by trying to hit his second shot all the way back to the flag instead of leaving it underneath the hole like he knew he should have. He hit it over the green and missed a short putt for par.

He ended up in a playoff with Nick Faldo. On the first hole of the playoff, number 10, Hoch hit a perfect drive and second shot in the middle of the green, while Faldo hit it in a greenside bunker and made bogey. Hoch had to two-putt an uphill 20-footer for the win. He ran his first putt two and a half feet past the hole and had a downhill left-to-right breaking putt for the win. He recalled that on the 17th hole, he had backed off his short par putt, which he missed. On the playoff hole, he said that he wanted to hit the breaking putt firmly, so as to eliminate most of the break, but he was not comfortable over the ball and knew that he was aiming too far to the left for the speed he wanted to hit the putt with. He said that he did not want to back off again because of what happened on 17, so he continued on. Everything seemed to be going too fast. He ultimately hit the putt too hard for where he was aiming and missed the putt that would have won him the tournament. He then lost the playoff on the next hole.

Analysis: The emotional anxiety of potentially winning led him to hit his shot on 15 farther. The emotional memory of the putt on 17th compromised his ability to hit the putt harder on the playoff hole. High negative emotions redirected his neuropathways (thinking routes in the brain) so everything appears faster as fewer options are explored. **The challenge was not physical, it was mental/emotional.**

> ➢ In the 1970 British Open at St. Andrews, Doug Sanders had a two-foot putt on the 18th green to beat Jack Nicklaus by a shot. Sanders said that, over the final three holes, he was already thinking that he had won the tournament and how great it was. On his two-footer on 18, Sanders took an inordinately long amount of time over the ball. Before he took the putter back, he was distracted by what he thought was a small pebble between his ball and the hole. He bent down to pick it up, only to realize that it was just a piece of discolored grass. Instead of going through his normal routine again, he went straight back to his stance over the ball. He said he could hear people in the gallery laughing and he thought to himself, "I'll teach them to laugh at me," instead of thinking about his putt, which he ended up missing. He lost a playoff to Nicklaus the next day and never won a single major championship.

Analysis: Hitting a two-foot putt was not the issue. Allowing his focus to wander was. **The challenge was not physical, it was mental/emotional.**

> ➢ In the 1961 Masters, Arnold Palmer was leading Gary Player by one shot when he hit his drive to the middle of the fairway on 18. It was going to be his third Masters in four years. His good friend, George Low, was in the gallery at the spot of his second shot and congratulated him on his victory. Palmer proceeded to hit his shot into the greenside bunker and make a double bogey to lose to Player by a shot. In many interviews Palmer has given since regarding that loss, he regrets how

his emotions got the better of him with the congratulatory comment.

Analysis: Even for the most talented and skilled golfers, vulnerability to unwelcome emotions and thoughts is high. The racing thoughts in his head over-powered the ability to hit the desired shot. **The challenge was not physical, it was mental/emotional.**

> In the 1999 British Open at Carnoustie, Jean Van de Velde held a three-shot lead on the 18th tee. Knowing that he only needed a double bogey to win, Van de Velde hit a driver off the tee instead of a 3-wood or even a long iron for safety. He hit it so far to the right that he luckily avoided the water hazard to the right of the fairway and ended up on the 17th hole. When the camera man zoomed in on his face after the tee shot, Van de Velde put his hand over the lens in embarrassment. After the fortunate break off the tee, he merely needed to pitch the ball back to the fairway and then play to the green from there. He later said that he did not want to win that way, by pitching back to the fairway, and instead wanted to win with a flare by hitting a 2-iron over the hazard in front of the green. His 2-iron flew into the grandstand to the right of the green, ricocheted off a metal pole, hopped off the rock wall of the hazard, and buried itself in a miserable lie in the waist high rough, still not over the water yet. Again, instead of pitching the ball sideways, he tried to go over the hazard, but did not hit it hard enough and hit it right in the middle of the water. After a drop, a pitch that found the front bunker, and a bunker shot, he ended up having to make a 7-footer for triple bogey just to get into a three-man playoff, which he eventually lost.

Analysis: Pitching the ball back in play was the right *cognitive* decision with the lead he had. His emotional desire to look heroic in victory trumped an otherwise simple decision. **The challenge was not physical, it was mental/emotional.**

➤ In the 2016 Masters, Ernie Els was playing his first hole of the first round. After missing the green and chipping up to three feet, Els experienced one of the worst cases of the yips that have ever been seen. Just the previous week in Houston, he had led the field in putting from inside of 10 feet. His stroke on the first green was so shaky and violent that he never even came close to hitting the hole on his 3-footer. He did the same thing on the comeback attempt from two feet and ended up missing three more times from less than three feet. He ended up six-putting the hole for a score of nine, and ultimately missed the cut. He admitted after the round that his game coming into the week was very sharp and he put a lot of pressure on himself to win a tournament that he desperately wanted to win in the late stages of his career.

Analysis: With each miss, it was less about a two-foot putt and more about the emotion of failure which diluted his focus on a routine putt. **The challenge was not physical, it was mental/emotional.**

➤ At the second stage of the 2012 PGA Tour Qualifying Tournament, a mini-tour player had finally gotten off to a solid start at the stage that had been his stumbling block to getting back out onto a major tour. This was the last year in which players could play their way straight onto the PGA Tour, but still with the consolation prize of assuring membership on the Web.com Tour. Through two rounds, he was nine under par and had only made a single bogey.

As he sat in the hotel room that evening, his mind started thinking ahead to how great it would be to at least get back out on the Web.com Tour, where he had not played since 2007. He was well inside the cut number and playing nearly flawlessly, so he was essentially planning his schedule out for the next year.

He was paired with two high profile players in the third round and felt like his brain was in a cloud all day. He was caught up in comparing his game to theirs and began hitting poor shot after poor shot. He shot 74 in the third round to put himself on the cut line. He was again paired with two notable players in the last round, and was again playing in a mental fog. He shot 75 in the final round to miss advancing.

Analysis: **There are three competitors in golf in this order: (i) you, (ii) the course, and (iii) other golfers**. The emotions of playing with two better-known players reversed the order of importance and focus. **The challenge was not physical, it was mental/emotional.**

> ➤ In the 1991 Ryder Cup at the Ocean Course at Kiawah Island, Mark Calcevecchia was playing against Colin Montgomery in the Sunday singles matches. Calcavecchia was four up with four to play and knew that even a half point either way could win or lose the Cup. Montgomery won the 15th and 16th holes, but hit his tee shot in the water on the par-three 17th. Needing only to hit the ball on dry land, Calcavecchia topped his tee shot into the water. After both dropped and played to the green, Calcavecchia needed a two-footer for a double bogey that would tie the hole and win the match. He missed the putt and lost the 18th hole as well to end up halving the match. After suffering what appeared to be a panic attack in the minutes following the match, Calcavecchia said that he had suddenly felt the entire weight of winning the Ryder Cup for his teammates when he was '4 up with 4 to play' and it became too big for him.

Analysis: The "weight" he is talking about is nothing more than the extreme emotional condition of that moment. The mistake was not in feeling that, but rather in not knowing how to deal with it. **The challenge was not physical, it was mental/emotional.**

> ➤ A junior golfer had an AJGA tournament where several college coaches would be in attendance. She had been playing very well

and had a great practice before the round. To her surprise, when she walked up to the first tee, virtually all the coaches were there even though several groups had already started before her. She had played in front of people before, but she said she had never felt so many eyes on her and became aware that every single thing she did on that tee box would be analyzed. She proceeded to block her shot out of bounds and never recovered. For the remainder of the round, she was more anxious to finish and get out than to try to recover and salvage a decent score.

Analysis: Her issue on the tee box had nothing to do with all the practice she had done on her physical game. She told me later she never practiced for a moment like that and had no idea how to process all that stimuli in her head. **The challenge was not physical, it was mental/emotional.**

➢ In the 1996 Masters, Greg Norman held a six-shot lead going into the last round. The Masters was always the tournament that he wanted to win the most, but it was also where he had suffered the most crushing defeats of his career in years past. He had played flawlessly in the first round, tying the course and major championship record of 63. His play had become more ragged over the next two rounds, but most analysts were still practically conceding him the tournament with 18 holes to go. In an interview almost 20 years later, Norman admitted that when he woke up Sunday morning, he could sense that he was "off". He said that he was struggling with an off the course issue that was on the verge of boiling over, yet he never told anyone about it. On the range before the round, he admitted that he was panicking, despite his coach and caddie both telling him his swing looked perfect. On the course, he opened with a bogey and made mistake after mistake, eventually shooting 78 and losing by five shots to Nick Faldo.

Analysis: We are human beings with one brain. There is no way to compartmentalize personal life from golf as it is the same brain that houses all experiences and memories. Personal life has arguably the largest emotional impact on a golfer because golf is a non-reactive sport (unlike basketball or tennis) where most of the time (93%) is not on the physical game. **The challenge was not physical, it was mental/emotional.**

> ➢ In the 2016 Masters, Jordan Spieth was attempting to become the fourth player in history to win back to back tournaments, as well as his third major championship. During the final round, Spieth made four consecutive birdies from holes 6 to 9 to open up a five-shot lead with nine holes to play. After playing his most solid nine holes of the tournament, Spieth later said that he started the back nine just trying to make pars to protect his lead. He began to hit poor shot after poor shot and made two bogeys in a row before hitting his tee shot in the water on number 12. After taking his drop, he proceeded to chunk his third shot into the water again and made a quadruple bogey. He ultimately lost the tournament by three shots. When later asked what his thinking was during those shots in the water, he said, "I don't know what I was thinking. It was a tough 30 minutes that I hope I never experience again."

Analysis: "Not being able to think clearly" is the sure sign that emotions have taken over, not that you cannot think. Managing emotions well is determined by how quickly you can think clearly again after a bad shot. **The challenge was not physical, it was mental/emotional.**

> ➢ In 2014, a new reality show came out, called *The Short Game*. The show documented a group of junior golfers, ages 7 to 9, and their parents, as they prepared for and competed in tournaments around the country. In most of the cases, a parent would caddie for the child during the competition and would very often harshly criticize and yell at the child after he or she made the first mistake of the round. This more often than not would trigger a tailspin of worse shots by the child and

even harsher criticism from the parent, leaving the child in tears before the round was even over. The children in those situations never showed any signs of improvement during the season and often appeared to resent the game as well.

Analysis: Experiences are stories told using words in monologues in our minds. Each carries an emotional value especially from people of importance in our lives. For kids and young adults, golf is mostly emotional as what it means to self-esteem and acceptance by others matters more. **The challenge was not physical, it was mental/ emotional.**

Clearly, there are hundreds more of these kinds of stories that can be shared. And it is not just in golf.

Other Sports

Athletes from all sports experience similar surprises, setbacks, and losses that are not attributable to the athlete's physical or technical skills. What must be noted in these other sports and athletes is that the common thread is how all athletes are, first, human beings built with the same physiology and neurology, and exhibiting the same emotional responses as golfers.

> A basketball player practices free throws thousands of times and makes all of them, yet something is different when the free throw has to be made with one second to go and the game is on the line. What is different? Is it the size of the basketball? The size of the rim? The distance to the basket? Did the basketball player suddenly lose weight or get shorter or lose 20 IQ points? No, of course not. What is different is the pressure of the situation – the emotions of the situation. This is not physical, it is emotional.

> At an Ironman event, a pro athlete was leading the race until about mile 16 of the run when another pro athlete passed him.

He had led the entire race and was shocked to get caught. So disheartened was he by this, that he decided to try to keep up with the new leader and go faster than he knew he could. Intellectually, he knew that he could not keep up the faster pace this late in the race but chose to ignore this, and push himself even harder. By mile 22, he was spent, and instead of a certain second place finish, he ended up 12th. After the race, he was visibly upset. He just could not understand why he reacted the way he did when he got passed, why he abandoned his race strategy and how he let his emotions at the time cause him to ignore his training, and instead, adopt a totally unrealistic running pace. He clearly underperformed and it had little to do with his physical skills.

➢ A NASCAR driver and his crew chief tell me that the race is called and raced differently in the first 200 laps versus the last 50 laps. The difference between the winner and the next 10 drivers is literally seconds, so the last 50 laps are critical for finishing position. But the track is the same as it was in the first 200 laps. What is different is the pressure of those last laps where critical decisions are made. Those last laps are no longer about cars and all about the decisions the driver and crew chief make. It is not about the equipment, but the emotions of the situation.

➢ A professional tennis player tells me the difference between the first four sets and the fifth set is just one thing: mental strength. She says it almost ceases to be about tennis, and whoever can remain calm in the moment of pressure and execute the shots they know they have hit thousands of times before in the fifth set almost always wins. What is the difference between the sets? What is different is the pressure of the situation – the emotions of the situation.

➤ The New York Knicks had a 105-99 lead with just 18.7 seconds left before Indiana Pacers' guard, Reggie Miller, sent them falling into one of the most stunning end-game collapses in NBA history by scoring 8 points in nine mind-blowing seconds. Miller began by hitting a 3-pointer. Then he stole the ensuing inbounds pass and dashed back out to the 3-point line, where he wheeled and drained another 3 points to tie the game at 105. "We were shell-shocked, we were numb," Knicks forward Anthony Mason remembered years later. "We became totally disoriented." The Knicks still had a few more chances to win, but John Starks missed two free throws, and Knicks center, Patrick Ewing, missed a 10-footer before Miller was fouled on the rebound. He made both free throws to give the Pacers a shocking 107-105 win, and then he ran off the Madison Square Garden floor yelling, "Choke artists!" The Pacers went on to win the series in seven games.

– Johnette Howard

Terms like "shell-shocked" and "disoriented," used by the Knicks and so many other athletes in all sports to describe how they felt, are lay terms, in effect conceding that *something* happened to them that they cannot explain. For any athlete, golf or other sport, there should be no part of his or her performance that he or she should not be prepared for, much less not be able to explain.

It should be noted that there is a fundamental difference between these kinds of stories of underperformance and others where athletes underperform because of physical reasons. If you have a strained back, it is going to be tough to hit the shots you know you can hit no matter how much emotional strength you have. When something irreparable happens to your body, no amount of EQ can compensate for that. Similarly, if you do not have the skill to do something in practice, then no amount of mental strength can create that skill on the golf course. If you do not have a high draw in your repertoire and never hit that shot successfully on the range, you simply cannot "will" yourself to do it.

As a neuro-sports psychologist, I have found that disappointment and frustration do not come from failing to execute on something never done before. They come from **underperformance, the inability to execute on the very things you have done many times before, but not when in matters most: during game time**. It is the examples given above that are much harder to swallow because you feel it was something *mental*, and the root cause of your poor reaction is still inexplicably a mystery to you. In these underperforming situations, you feel like you *lost* control and let something derail you. You feel like you beat yourself. This is where neuroscience and EQ can make a tremendous difference.

"What separates great players from the good ones is not so much ability as brain power and emotional equilibrium." -Arnold Palmer

So Why Train in EQ?

As described above, rounds of golf are littered with these stories of self-inflicted wounds where the mind inexplicably chose to make poor decisions *in the heat of battle* during 'game time', and in many cases, decisions that were contrary to what they and their coaches had already agreed on during training. Why did their minds deviate from their strategy? Why did they react in a manner where, in hindsight, and with a much clearer mind, they would have all made different and better decisions? What is it about golfers' emotions during anxiety situations that shut down very logical decision-making, decisions that they can make on any other day without blinking an eye? What could they have done during practice to prepare them for the "heat of the battle" scenarios?

In all sports, if athletes are able to maintain composure, access their training memories, and simply perform as they have trained, then their chances of being successful go up significantly. This is obvious. How to do it is not so obvious. ***This is why we train in EQ.*** We need to understand exactly how our brain works and what our brain is doing in those situations so that we can change it. Arguably the worst feeling an athlete can have is performing poorly during game time and have no idea what is going on in his or her mind and body. We need to prepare ourselves to stay focused and positive in the midst of surprises and distractions so that we can perform our best - be it on the golf course or in everyday experiences.

The reality is that golf is a game of surprises.

Since golf is full of surprises, and surprises are processed in the brain, it is, therefore, a game of mental/emotional strength. This is a learnable skill, like any other, and is required 100% of the time you are playing golf, be it over a shot or in between shots. This fundamental shift in reframing how you view and play golf is the first step in building your Golf EQ and using the GYRA Scorecard.

I define mental/emotional strength as the ability to recognize and convert negative thoughts/emotions to positive ones.

Note that mental/emotional strength is different from being in a zone. I will discuss the latter in the next chapter. My contention is that not only can these surprises be managed differently during a round, but in fact, you can effectively train for them and increase your EQ. It is impossible to predict what is going to go wrong and when it will happen, but suffice it to say, in all likelihood something will happen that will cause anxiety just before or during your round. This we can all agree on. And if you concede this, then, in order to perform at your best on game day and hit a shot that counts, your practice must prepare you to manage your emotions and thoughts.

A plan that incorporates mental training will help you manage the unpredictable but certain to occur anxiety-inducing experiences, and your responses to them. As noted in the introduction, if you are going to spend so much time and money desperately searching for a perfect swing and shot, why not spend just a few minutes a day to grow your

EQ and remain positive and focused in the throes of situations that are beyond your control? No one wishes for chaos of any kind during a round, but **a positive recovery from a bad situation can actually be incredibly motivating and powerful to spur you on to an even better performance.**

"Competitive golf is played mainly on a five-and-a-half-inch court, the space between your ears." -Bobby Jones

Please take a few moments to write down in your own words an experience where you underperformed in a round, similar to the stories shared earlier in this chapter. In subsequent chapters, as tools are shared, you will be asked to come back to this story and personalize your learning. By writing down your own personal experiences, your own emotions and presence in the experience will make the learning and subsequent growth a much richer endeavor. As you write your story, try to describe yourself emotionally, mentally, and physically, as well as the situation you were in as graphically as you can.

Note that a surprise is not just a situation where something has gone terribly wrong, like the stories described earlier, but surprises can be anything where you have lost your focus and as a result, deviated from your capabilities and underperformed.

Exercise:
My Personal Story of Under-Performing

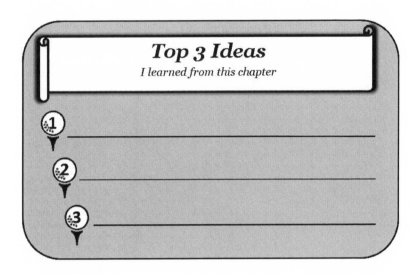

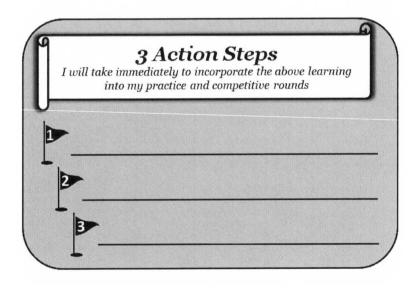

Chapter Summary

1. Surprises are bound to occur on every round. They happen to all golfers – professionals and amateurs.

2. When surprises happen, our emotions and thoughts are tested, more so than golf skills. This test occurs in the brain.

3. Failure to not know what is happening in the brain, as shown in this chapter, is what leads to performing well below your capability.

Chapter 2

- *Consider that our well-intentioned bronze-age elders conjured labels for emotions because they had virtually no understanding of how our brain actually worked. Those labels - emotional language - are outdated yet we still use them. What you feel is worth understanding better.*
- *Muscles do not have memory. They do not create, store, retrieve memories/learned skills. ALL of it happens ONLY in the brain. So don't "force" your muscles to remember by over training/practice. Invest time (training hours) in learning how YOUR brain can execute learned skills.*
- *You're only as good as your most negative thoughts.*

@izzyjustice

Neuroscience of a Golfer

It is critical that you understand how your brain works physiologically. Your brain is the ultimate equipment in your round. If you can spend hours in the gym, shell out thousands of dollars on equipment like your clubs, and spend years perfecting the golf swing, then consider spending quality time on understanding your brain as a piece of equipment that you need to appreciate with the same level of passion and detail. Unlike the 14 clubs you are playing with, however, your brain (emotions and thoughts) is constantly changing, which makes understanding it even more important. Imagine playing with 14 clubs that change in shaft or grip or lie angle after each shot. That would be crazy and a recipe for disaster. Yet, that is exactly what is happening to your thoughts and emotions after each shot – they are constantly changing. **The most important equipment that you use on every shot, your brain, is constantly changing!**

Recall what I shared earlier, when a golfer comes to see me, one of the first questions I ask him or her is to describe his or her favorite club to me. If it is a driver, the golfer will describe in infinite detail the shaft length, flex, club head size and materials, grip, and so much more. After the detailed description, I pause and then ask for a description of his or her brain. I get the same reaction you just had: "Huh?"

If all the decisions are made in only one part of your body — and that is your brain — then of all the tools and skills to master, knowing your brain and how it works is the singular most important skill all golfers, amateurs and professionals alike, should invest in.

How many decisions do you have to make in a round of golf? Please take a few moments to do the following exercise.

Exercise:

Decisions Made in a Round of Golf

Make a list of the most common cognitive decisions you have to make in a round of golf.

1.

2.

3.

4.

5.

6.

7.

8.

9.

10.

There are probably another 10 you can easily come up with. As you can see, there are numerous decisions to be made in a round of golf, and they are all made in and by only one part of your body: your brain.

Brain Background

The ultimate goal for you is to perform at your best on the course when it matters. Not on the range and not during practice rounds, but when it matters most – during game time – when every shot really counts. Period. Once you are physically ready (training), and as discussed in many examples in Chapter 1, good and timely decision-making, which only occurs in the brain (not in your grip, elbows, hips, or spine angle) is at the heart of optimal performance, where you are able to perform these physical skills. Decision-making, therefore, is a key piece to optimal performance because without it, you are guaranteed to underperform. All decisions are made in the brain. Period.

We are currently living in the Golden Age of Neuroscience – the study of the brain. The first human anatomy of significance was done by a Belgian physician (Andreas Vesalius) in 1514. That is only about 500 years ago. It was not until 1985 that a Dutch physician (Willem Einthoven) invented the ECG/EKG machine to track electrical activity in the brain, and he won a Nobel Prize for it. And not until we built digital scanning technology were we able to map the human brain, just in the last 20 years. Because the brain sits heavily protected by the skull, it has never been easy to access without irreparable damage, until now. The software term I used earlier is also mostly electric waves travelling very fast. **Our brain really has been the mysterious frontier of exploration of humankind**. Keep in mind that what I am sharing with you here is profoundly new evidence in the search for both understanding the brain and optimal human performance (getting the mind and body to perform optimally on demand). I could write a book on the brain, and there are dozens already written by my peers, but this book is about taking complex research and converting it into usable knowledge for you, the golfer.

Key Brain Facts:

1. The brain works in brain waves – billions of electric waves traveling through roads (neuropathways) taking information from one place to another to make sense of stimuli and formulate a response.
2. The brain performs primarily two key functions:
   a. Records and stores experiences (library)
   b. Makes decisions (commander in chief)

3. The purpose to record and store experiences is so that those experiences can be used to make future decisions.

4. 80% to 95% of all decisions are subconscious. This means you are mostly not in control (conscious) of what you are thinking/doing.

5. The brain is "wandering" on average 65% of the time. This means that 65% of the time your mind is not where your body is.

6. The state that we call "being in the zone" – when we perform our best without really knowing why – is when there are essentially only two very low frequency brain waves traveling in the brain: alpha and theta waves (4-12 Hz).

7. Alpha waves lead to calm and sound decision-making. We will call this being **AGNOSTIC (A).** This is where the default 80% to 95% of *subconscious* decision-making is considerably lower and you are more *conscious* of what you want to do.

8. Theta waves lead to feeling a calm sense of presence in a moment in time. This is where the default 65% of mind-wandering is considerably lower. We will learn a new emotional language using colors here: **Green (G), Yellow (Y), and Red (R).** Collectively, this is the GYR of the GYRA Scorecard.

Every athlete wants to perform in "the zone." Athletes know what this experience is like. A state of quiet, calm, thought-free, and full command of what you want to do with the club or ball (conscious). Golfers can describe their rounds of being in a zone in vivid detail. There are no thoughts of swing mechanics, consequences, monologues, commentaries … just a state of being. It is important to acknowledge that this 'zone' state is a neurological state, not an athletic (neuromuscular or technique) one. When I ask them how they got there, there is bewilderment. When I ask them how they will get there again, there is even more bewilderment.

Now that we know scientifically what types of brain waves constitute being in the zone, alpha and theta waves, we can build skills (GYRA) to measure (without a brain scan) those waves and then make adjustments to get back to the zone brain waves. Without getting into a neuroscience type book, let us understand each fact better.

The brain works in brain waves – billions of electric waves traveling through roads (neuropathways) taking information from one place to another to make sense of stimuli.

All our technology uses electric or sound waves of some sort. They travel in a frequency of current measured in hertz, named after German physicist, Heinrich Hertz (1857-1894). Because of this, only until recently have we been able to track specific waves per experience. If we show you a picture of a beautiful flower, we can measure the frequency of that wave, we can track where it goes, from what part of the brain meaning is derived, and the subsequent impact of that meaning to the rest of the neuromuscular body. If we show you a picture of a car accident, we can track that, too, all the way through.

For golf, we can measure the kinds of waves when trying to make a three-foot putt for par versus a three-foot putt to save bogey. Furthermore, we can actually predict the kinds of waves in each type of situation. **We know the difference in brain activity when hitting a 150-yard shot with no hazards in play versus the same shot with hazards in play. The same shot is being processed by completely different brain waves. The shot with all the hazards has considerably more brain waves (quantity) and their intensity is higher (Hz) because the memories used to make sense of a hazard are negative, not positive.** This shot is far away from the low intensity zone alpha and theta brain waves.

The ability of the golfer to make an effort to get alpha and theta waves, fewer and slower frequency waves, is therefore critical to executing a golf shot because the neuromuscular ability to do so rests entirely on the frequency of the current of the decision from the brain to the muscles.

The brain performs primarily two key functions:

a. **Records and stores experiences (library)**
b. **Makes decisions (commander in chief)**

Virtually all experiences are recorded and stored. The brain is designed to do this. If you experienced or learned that a lion eats people, then at any point in the future, if you see a lion, in person or in a movie perhaps, then your brain will take the visual stimulus of the lion, search its library, and ascribe meaning to it. In golf, if you played a hole poorly on one day, rest assured you will remember what you did on that hole the next time you play it. That previous memory will cause frequencies to increase and more waves to be present as you know you do not want to duplicate the mistake. In this regard, our brain is not our friend.

It is also a myth to "have a short memory." There is no such thing. In fact, trying to intentionally forget something negative, neurologically has the opposite and worse effect of actually increasing waves (thoughts) and their frequencies. I get the reasoning for "having short memory" in sports, but it is the wrong approach. Later in the book, I will show you how to deal with these negative thoughts.

There are some fundamental problems with how our brain is designed, in terms of memory storage.

1. Our brain does not store positive and negative memories the same way. This is something we have only recently learned. If 10 things happened to you yesterday and nine of them were amazing, but one of them you burned the tip of your finger while making coffee, today, the next day, you are likely to talk about (consciously) the burned finger more than the nine good experiences, and subconsciously, just the smell of coffee anywhere will likely trigger a heightened sense of alert and precautionary safety behavior. In golf, you are more likely to remember the bad shots you hit than the good ones, and worse,

you will remember the bad one at the most inopportune time. This will take our brain waves farther from those alpha and theta waves we want.

2. Up until about 100 or so years ago, most humans never travelled more than 50 miles from where they were born. The amount of stimuli to process and store was infinitely less than today, where we literally carry thousands of stimuli with us wherever we go with our mobile devices. Our brain is not designed to process the sheer volume of this stimuli. In addition, our ancestors took several naps (circadian rhythm) during the day and week. These 'sleep' times were critical for the brain to resurface its roads (neuropathways) and store the right experiences in the right part of the brain. I will discuss this in a later chapter, but note for now that our brains and our current lifestyle are not designed to hit a golf shot in an alpha and theta (zone) state. We bring dozens of conscious and subconscious commentators to each shot.

These two flaws make requiring a deeper understanding of the brain a must-have skill, as the challenges are becoming more and more mental and less physical.

The second function of the brain is to make decisions. Your brain processes the lie of a shot, what the wind is doing, where the pin is, what trouble there might be, where the safe miss is, and so on, before making a decision on what shot to hit. No surprise here. Unfortunately, there are a few problems here, too.

1. Because the brain that makes decisions is also the library, and has to be, it is like having the wolf in the hen house. All competitions are pressure situations. Later in the book, I will give you the neurological definition of pressure. In pressure situations, our brain relies more on the negative storage library than the positive one. When trying to make the same three-foot putt for bogey, the brain will likely remember a recent

missed putt more so than a recent made putt. This default mechanism is not helpful to making the putt at hand as negative memories carry very high frequencies with them, the opposite of those desired alpha and theta low frequency waves.

2. Speed kills. Higher frequencies of brain waves, often used for full swings and high intensity experiences, impact 'speed calibration' especially in the short game. How hard or soft to hit a putt, chip, pitch, or bunker shot is a neurological output. If you want to hit a shot soft, it will be very difficult to do so when frequencies in the brain are high. We call this golf skill as "having good touch" where the reality is that this phrase has more to do with brain waves than the sensation of touch.

Again, the key message here is that if you understand how the brain works so that you may change it to alpha and theta waves while over a ball, then the moment of truth will have a significant advantage over others, because you will be able to get your brain to do what you have physically trained to do and are capable of.

The purpose to record and store experiences is so that those experiences can be used to make future decisions.

Artificial intelligence (AI) is essentially technology that tries to mimic what the brain does. It is algorithms with very high levels of predictive analytics. If you go online to your favorite store to buy a pair of golf pants, for example, and you pick the size of the pants, predictive analytics can guess what else you might want to buy based on thousands of similar purchases or based on your profile data, such as how much you typically spend when buying things online. The AI will show you on your screen a matching belt, golf shirt, and hat, and offer a discount if purchased together. Our actual brain is no different. In order to make sense of any stimuli, it researches its own library to assess all possible data similar to the original stimulus. It has to do this because this is, in fact, what intelligence is – the ability to make the best decision on how to respond to a stimulus. We call this *experience*.

If you have an uphill putt, the stimuli of the slope and grain is given meaning based on past experiences that indicate you have to hit the putt more firmly. It would be silly to have a brain that processed all stimuli with an objective perspective and being forced to learn all over again. Our brain is designed to avoid this relearning.

There are, however, a couple of key problems with this kind of software for golfers.

1. If all current experiences are based on what is in our memory, and it is, then our brain is essentially a very biased commentator or interpreter. This is why we interpret new experiences based on our past experiences, not as they are, not objectively.

    This is a hard pill to swallow, to accept that all we know is based on what we know and not on what is actually objective. I would argue that *what we do not know about what we know is much larger than what we do know*. For golfers making decisions on the course during competition, this is a terrible bias. Every shot is based on previous shots. If you start your round hitting it left, you are likely to start aiming right on subsequent shots. If you have been leaving putts short, you are likely to hit next putts harder, even if the putt did not warrant a firmer stroke. Experience and past memories are good in the example above on the uphill putt; yes, you need to remember to hit it more firmly, but you do not need to remember the last putt that you missed. This leads to the second problem.

2. Under pressure of any kind (I will define pressure later), the brain is designed to remember its negative memories more than its positive ones. All golfers can attest to being over a shot and inexplicably remember something negative from a previous

hole or suddenly be more aware of the water on the left. Our brain is designed to do just this. If you are hiking and hear a loud roar from an animal, our brain is designed to sound the neurological alarm system and cause us to stop and run in the opposite direction. In this pressure situation, we must run. Our brain decides that sounds like these are dangerous and harmful to us. Our brain does not want us to be calm and have those alpha and theta waves. It wants the opposite – high intensity, irrational fast action to run. In this scenario, it is doing the right thing.

Over a putt to save par, a different pressure situation, the brain uses the same software to react the same way, resulting in tension and increase in probability of missing the putt. To the brain, there is no difference between the threat of a wild animal and the threat of missing a putt. The same system is activated. This is good during the hike, but not good during golf, making the brain both friend and foe. It is why golf is really a battle between you and you.

80% to 95% of all decisions are subconscious. This means you are not in control (conscious) of what you are thinking/ doing.

This has been one of the more astounding discoveries of the human brain. It is unbelievable at first, so let us spend some time studying this. First, there are thousands of physiological decisions that the brain is making that we are simply not conscious of because they happen too routinely or quickly. When we walk, do we count the distance between each step to make sure it is a certain distance, or does our body have a geo-spatial mechanism to understand balance and know that steps too big are 'not comfortable' and automatically make the adjustment? When we sit, do we consciously decide where our glutes will land, where our knees, feet, arms, and other parts come to rest? How do you know you are hungry? Or thirsty? Or cold? Or tired? Or sleepy? Or to blink your eyes? Or to breathe? Or read with comprehension? **All these decisions have to be subconsciously done because the volume is simply too high to consciously do.** We save our conscious decisions for what to say in a conversation, what to write, what to wear, what to eat, etc. Conscious decisions are a lot, too, but are usually paced well apart in time, though no way close to the volume of subconscious decisions. Even many of the decisions we believe are conscious are actually subconscious. When you are over a putt, and suddenly recall a similar missed putt, clearly you did not intend (conscious) to remember the missed putt. No golfer I know intends to hit a bad shot, yet hits them all the time. Clearly the signal from the brain between what we want to do (conscious) and what we end up doing (bad shot) did not happen by accident. Your body did it. It came from somewhere within you. **There is no random in the brain.** There might be numerous actions, behaviors, emotions, and thoughts we do not understand, but none are random. We may not consciously know the reason, but there is a reason, and it is largely from our subconscious.

The best way I have explained this to golfers is to imagine that you are about to make a swing and you feel great about the shot. You know what type of shot to hit and you have hit similar shots many times before. On your downswing, some other person near you says, "Don't hit it left," and you mis-hit the shot. This is easy to rationalize. Someone else caused a distraction that your brain had to adjust to. In that moment, the electric signal that needed to travel from your brain to your muscles to execute the shot was compromised because your brain had to process a new stimulus of some dude suddenly yelling during your downswing. **This is, in effect, exactly what our own brains do to us**, largely led by the negative memories that the subconscious retrieves to protect us from a competitive danger (similar to another person saying something to you). **Your subconscious is your true competitor.** It is where the library and decision-making are. The "wolf in the hen house" is a very accurate metaphor. In competition, if not managed, the subconscious will self-select mostly negative memories to "yell in your swing" and this will activate your subconscious, leading to a mis-hit. That yell is similar to hearing the roar during the hike, where you just ran. Same software.

In golf, the dichotomy between what you consciously want to do (hit a shot the way you want to and are capable of) and the subconscious interpretation of the same situation, is a very real battle and a sport all of its own. Golf is a non-reactionary sport. There is no one playing defense against you trying to stop you, and it is an endurance sport played over four or five hours. Both these attributes are fertilizer for the subconscious and why all the greats in this sport have said that this game is really a battle between you and you. In the next few chapters, you will learn how to win this battle. You will learn to reduce the role of the subconscious and increase the role of the conscious (increase the success of what you want to do.)

The brain is wandering on average 65% of the time. This means that 65% of the time, your mind is not where your body is.

In yet another one of the more astounding findings is this fact. Harvard professor, Matt Killingsworth, conducted the study (his findings can be viewed in his TED Talk on YouTube). For golf, an endurance sport, the consequences of mind wandering are quite staggering. If you are over a ball getting ready to hit a shot and your mind is processing a breakup with your loved one, or a death of a loved one, or what you will do after the round, or what you did the night before, or thousands of other possible thoughts aided by the subconscious and natural disposition of the brain to recollect negative experiences versus positive ones in competition, you are going to hit a poor shot.

This troubling fact is largely responsible for underperformance not just in golf, but also in life. If you are not mentally where you are physically, how can you pay attention to what is happening or what someone is saying, solve problems, be present with your loved ones when you are with them, be curious about something so that you can learn, and allow the brain to grow? If you had a rough day at work and you are having dinner with your family, but your mind is still replaying all the events of the rough day, how could you possibly hear and react to conversations happening around you to the best of your ability?

Mind wandering is a key fertilizer for the subconscious as it allows for it to take over the conscious part of the brain. If your brain outside of golf is mind wandering at this rate (65%), and because it is the same software, then the number of brain waves (volume) is too high for the alpha and theta waves to surface. It is foolish to think you can muscle your way to focusing, when off the course you cannot do the same. In this regard, a key component of being successful on the golf course is training in **mindfulness** (opposite of mind wandering) off the golf course. If the mind wanders to negative memories or scenarios as the brain is designed to do in competition, the intensity of the brain waves increases dramatically, making it difficult to bring them back down to the lower levels. It is the cause of "losing your touch" in the short game.

Mind wandering is not just about negative memories or scenarios, but also positive ones. You could be over a shot and be thinking about a vacation you are getting ready to take, or an easy birdie or shot you think you are about to execute, or winning a tournament before even hitting a shot.

The term Agnostic (A) is critical to master. Literally, it means "free of," and in this context, it means free of the past or the future. Both the past (what has happened before) and the future (what might happen) are neurological distractions, similar to someone else saying something on your downswing.

Being agnostic is not the brain's default disposition. In 65% of average situations, it is not agnostic. It is wandering. The brain can be trained to be agnostic. The software of the brain can be changed. In the neuroscience world, we call this concept of changing the brain's software neuroplasticity. Many of the exercises and GYRA tools you will learn in the next few chapters are based on neuroplasticity.

> **The state that we call "being in the zone" – when we perform our best without really knowing why – is when there are essentially only two very low frequencies traveling in the brain: alpha and theta waves (4-12 Hz).**

Neuroscientists have been studying the brain waves in athletes when in a zone. Technology can allow for a helmet, cap, or a headband to be over the brain measuring athletes' waves when performing. Data can be captured when good shots are made and when bad ones are made. Athletes performing in the zone have predominantly low frequency brain waves called alpha and theta waves. To be in a zone, both the quantity of brain activity (or thoughts) and the intensity of those thoughts (frequency current) are low. This low frequency is required for high sensory function. **In other words, for your eyes to see the line of the putt, visualize a shot, have the right pressure on your grip, and have a proper sense of force, these low frequency brain waves are necessary.** From the previous neurological findings, this means that the subconscious decision-making is low (below 30%); which means that the conscious decision-making (doing what you intend to do) is higher (70%). Reducing mind wandering is, therefore, also a major success factor in order to be in a zone where alpha and theta waves can occur.

We can now define pressure in neurological terms.

Pressure is when there are too many thoughts and most of them are negative.

Pressure is the opposite of being agnostic. In pressure, the brain is processing both the past and the future, and mostly with a negative narrative driven by the subconscious. In pressure, the narrative can be dictated by the circumstances. You could be tied for the lead on the last hole. Your brain is now processing all kinds of thoughts, such as: "What if I lose? I need to make birdie. Don't make a mistake. Should I hit driver since I pulled my last drive? I have not been in this situation before. I need to win in order to get to the next step," and the like.

All these thoughts over this putt create multiple brain waves as each one comes from a memory, and in order to even have a thought, the brain has to retrieve past memories using other brain waves and transport these additional waves to another place (synapse) to meet yet other memories to create a thought. This is a lot of brain activity creating higher EKG readings (brain waves), and if there are any negative ones, perhaps a previous round in a similar situation where a bad shot was struck, (trauma), then the intensity of that wave associated with other waves creates what we commonly call pressure.

Two key points about this:

1. Pressure is a neurological condition where symptoms show up physically. Pressure creates poor shots, not because you do not know how to hit the shot, but because your brain while in pressure situation is non-agnostic.

2. If pressure is too many thoughts and most are negative, then in order to get out of pressure, you will need to simply reduce the number of thoughts (if you get to very low numbers, then theta waves can occur), and if they are mostly positive, then alpha waves can occur. You can train your brain to do this.

"Every time you lose, you think that life's unfair. You think of the bad breaks. But when you're winning and playing well, you still get those bad breaks, only you overcome them. It just depends on how strong your mind is." -Greg Norman

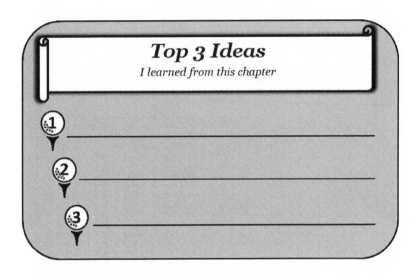

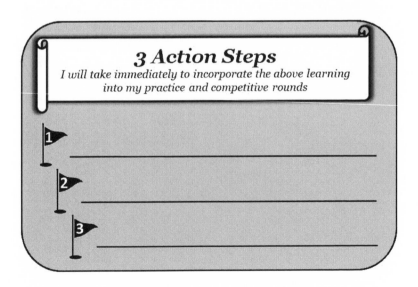

Chapter Summary

1. The brain works in brain waves, using neuropathways to send electrical waves that, in effect, are transporting information in order to make sense of a stimulus.
2. The brain primarily functions both as a library (records/stores experiences) and command center (makes decisions).
3. The purpose to record and store experiences is so that those experiences can be used to make future decisions.
4. 80%-95% of all decisions are subconscious, i.e. you are not in conscious control.
5. The brain is wandering on average 65% of the time.
6. "Being in the zone," is when there are essentially only two very low frequencies traveling in the brain, alpha and theta waves (4-12 Hz).
7. Alpha waves lead to calm and sound decision-making.
8. Theta waves lead to a calm sense of presence in a moment in time.
9. The GYR of the GYRA Scorecard uses the language of colors: Green (G), Yellow (Y), and Red (R).

Chapter 3

- *Emotional Accountant... do you have one? Someone that assigns an emotional cost to your experiences to gauge how much you have when you really need to perform at a high level? No? Well ... your brain subconsciously already does it - and it's very negatively biased.*
- *It is a convenient falsehood that you are as good as your strengths ... actually, you are as good as the weight of your weaknesses. Your strengths are mostly used to compensate for your weaknesses ... not to reach your full potential.*
- *When you learn to become comfortable playing well with your B game, your B games becomes pretty good!*

@izzyjustice

GYR – Golf EQ (Emotions)

Emotional Intelligence (EQ)

I wrote a book in 2015 on the role of emotions in golf. In the book, *Golf EQ, The Game Between Shots*, I shared the neurological model below of how decisions are made and the role of EQ.

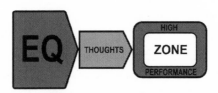

Figure 1. Neurological Sequence of Performance

What you see in Figure 1 is the neurological sequence in the brains of human beings for all decision-making, whether it is athletic or in day-to-day life. Emotions are the first neurological response by your brain and body to any given stimulus. Your physical body is an equipment that you want to manipulate correctly for a required shot. **Everything in your body and brain is dictated first by your emotions**. Emotions lead to thinking and dictate what type of thoughts, conscious or subconscious, you will have and how much mind wandering will occur.

Our five senses aggressively and constantly send signals to the prefrontal lobes of the brain located in our forehead area. This is the "port of entry" of all stimuli. Everything we see, hear, feel, touch, and smell gets sent here for primarily one purpose – to assign a threat rating to that experience. Happening in microseconds, the higher the threat level, the more the secretion of powerful hormones like cortisol (stress), which can cause high states of pressure. Sometimes this is emotionally labelled as fear, which is nothing more than a negative-outcome thought, a non-agnostic thought. There is no emotion (chemical) in our body called fear. The cortisol simply directs thoughts to negative sections of the brain library because, like hearing the animal roar during the hike, we have to make sense of the roar, and when in danger, the brain will take all actions necessary, including shutting down the conscious brain, to get you out of danger. In golf, while playing, this is a disaster. A poor shot has the same neurological impact as hearing the roar of an animal during a hike. The same chemicals are released. As a golfer, you feel like you do not even know what you are doing or how to do simple things and cannot figure out why or how you got there. You want it to end and get out. You can imagine the volume of thoughts and the intensity of the thoughts.

The lower the threat level, perceived or real, the fewer negative memories have to be used to make sense of the current situation, thereby reducing subconscious activity and mind wandering. A putt for birdie on the first hole of a tournament is not as threatening as a putt for birdie to make the cut, though both are one stroke each. The threat of the putt to make the cut is quite severe and the brain will do what it is designed to do, which is to activate the subconscious (pulling negative memories from the past).

"Of all the hazards, fear is the worst." -Sam Snead

The Biology of the Brain

Muscles do not have any memory cells or neuropathic abilities. **There is no such thing as muscle memory.** This term was created to simply justify hours of practice. Practice is good and essential to the learning process, but make no mistake that learning is ultimately stored in the brain, not muscles, and it is from the brain that the skill will have to be retrieved when playing. You can train your muscles and body parts for new motor skills, but in terms of the command to execute those new skills, that comes from the brain. A person in a coma whose body is perfectly normal is unable to perform any physical activity because the command center, the brain, is disabled.

From the command center, the brain, all orders are sent to different parts of the body. The body itself cannot do anything without the brain. The brain sends all its instructions through the spinal cord and what we call the nervous system, an integrated weave of nerves that carry the frequencies from the brain to the neuromuscular system. In other words, the spinal cord is like a bundle of cables for that critical information from memory banks to be sent to parts of your body. Now, as shown in the next image, conveniently located between the spinal cord and the brain — between the command center and cables — is the amygdala.

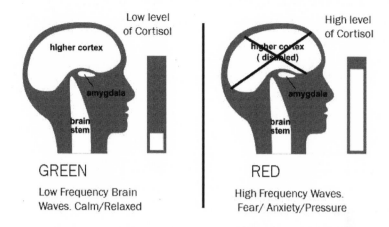

Figure 2. Impact of Emotions

The Instinctive Emotional Response

The amygdala is a gland that secretes hormones in your body, as described earlier. It is situated there because its job is to respond according to the directions of the prefrontal lobes – the threat center. The prefrontal lobes sit in your forehead area. Within microseconds of sensing a potential threat, the amygdala (and other glands, like the hippocampus) releases hormones in your body that either partially or entirely disables your brain. This disabling of cognitive functions enables your body to respond quickly and instinctively to that danger. This is essentially a safety mechanism, which is triggered as a reaction to every threat, regardless of whether the danger is perceived or real. *Our bodies have spent thousands of years morphing into this state so that we can perform our primary function – recognize danger and react to survive.* This is no different than most other living organisms. Although there are some universal physical dangers, such as someone pointing a gun at you, most emotional threats have no standards. It is different for everyone and based entirely on our past experiences, our memory banks, and mostly from our childhood or previous failures.

For example, if you are crossing a road and you see a car coming at you from the corner of your eye, you would, without thinking, instinctively jump or run to get the heck out of the way. You would not think about it; you would not analyze, "I wonder how fast the car is going? What are my options here?" If you did that, if you used the cognitive functions of your brain, you would not be able to respond fast enough and you would be hit. The brain has to be disabled quickly for you to instinctively jump out of the way of the car. No different from the roar example while hiking.

Similarly, because it is the same brain, cognitive functions are disabled when golfers get into situations that they perceive as danger, such as going to the first tee knowing all of a sudden you have gone from hitting inconsequential shots on the range to a very consequential shot. You can now begin to understand that no skill is lost between the range and first tee. What is different is the number of thoughts (quantity) of the changed stimuli of a fairway (versus a driving range) and the playing partners next to you. The physiological response in the body at the first tee is virtually identical to that of a car coming at us. In other words, the amygdala does not make the distinction between the threat of a car coming at us or hearing a roar in the woods, and the threat of the consequences of a bad first tee shot. They are both threats: one is physical and the other is emotional.

"Putts get real difficult the day they hand out the money." -Lee Trevino

Look at the body's physiological automatic and instinctive response to anything perceived as a negative experience, depicted in Figure 3. A negative experience is not really negative in an objective sense. It becomes negative (pressure) because, in order to make sense of the experience, negative memories have been retrieved, mostly subconsciously. In doing this without our conscious consent, the brain waves in quantity increase because a negative memory has so many layers to it, most of which were never fully understood or processed. In addition, and as a result, the electrical frequency (Hz) increases the intensity of those memories. All this is happening in seconds. In this state, just look at the impact of negative emotions on the physical body, the same body that you need to hit a golf shot. No athlete can perform at his or her best in this state. **This is akin to being physically injured!** In every round, as discussed earlier, a golfer is guaranteed to be in this state.

This physiological state leads to a high alert state, where the brain is operating in "lockdown mode," similar to the scenario of the speeding car approaching or the hiking roar. The following changes occur in this state:

- Decreased cognitive performance
- Less oxygen available for critical brain functions
- Tendency to over generalize
- Tendency to respond with defensive action
- Perception of small stressors as worse than they actually are
- Easily aggravated
- Recollection of past negative experiences
- Difficulty getting along with others
- Cannot perform at your best

The next image (Figure 3) shows what happens to the physiological body under the same circumstance. How can a golfer execute a good shot in this state?

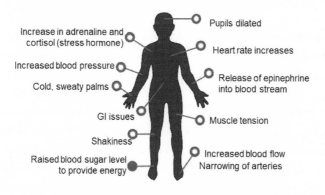

Figure 3. The Body's Auto-Responsive Physiology

This state leads to those negative monologues where we doubt our training, question our will, and recall past negative situations unintentionally. Negative monologues are rarely intentional. I do not meet many golfers who say they intended to have negative self-talk. Yet it happens all the time. This is a sign that your brain waves are operating at a high frequency. Those negative monologues are not random. **There is no random in the brain**. It is your brain actively retrieving negative memories to make sense of the current one. Sometimes, actual behavior can reveal this, too, like throwing a club or cursing. At that point, access to our rational ability and skill memory has been disabled and we are in the instinctive fight-or-flight mode. Again, no golfer can perform his or her best in this state. One simply is hijacked by one's own brain and body in the most natural and instinctive of ways. It is a virtual guarantee that every golfer will be in this state several times during a round. The question then becomes how to manage this state. This is where EQ and the GYRA scorecard come in.

"The object of golf is to beat someone. Make sure that someone is not yourself." -Bobby Jones

Negative Monologues

There is arguably no greater threat to an athlete than his or her own negative monologue. We all have them, not just in golf but in life as well. You know the ones where you talk to yourself about all the reasons why you cannot or should not do something, where you recall the worst memories, and seriously doubt in your ability to perform? There is no human being who actively pursues a negative monologue. They happen without choice, and very often at the most inopportune of times.

Conversely, athletes often say that when they are at their best, *in the zone*, that there is no such negative monologue. In fact, the calm state is almost euphoric as though everything is exactly how it should be and they are performing magic. You now know this is entirely neurological, where two low frequency waves are present in your brain, mind wandering is very low, and subconscious activity is also low.

In golf, an endurance sport of many hours, you are certain to have both types of dialogues. I will discuss at length how to manage your emotions and these dialogues, but it is important to understand how the negative ones, more harmful to your performance, are created.

Let us recall the example of accidentally touching a hot stove. Of the 10 experiences you may have had yesterday, nine were spectacular ones – very positive – but one of them was negative, where you may have accidentally touched a hot stove and slightly burnt your hand while making coffee. Today, the day after, which experience do you think you will be remembering more? If you answered honestly, then it would be the negative one, not the nine other great positive ones. Why? Once again, our physiological design and neurological construction from thousands of years takes center stage. Our brain has a specific place in the back of our skull where, in fact, negative memories are stored. When we have negative experiences in life, whether traumatic ones or like the slight hand burn, the brain needs to store them so that they can easily be retrieved. You *need* to remember the burnt hand more than the nine positive experiences because the burnt hand plays a larger role in your survival than your positive experiences. You need to remember to be careful next time you are near a hot stove.

In this manner, almost all of our life's negative experiences are not only permanently stored, but they are, in fact, the ones that are first retrieved if the prefrontal lobes (threat center of brain) label a current experience as a negative one (one with potential threat). So as the amygdala disables the brain in high anxiety situations after getting word from the prefrontal lobes, your cognitive functions (making decisions, remembering how to do routine skills) are further limited to those negative memories, and thus, the negative monologues.

A golfer who was nervous going to the first tee recalls that he remembered what another golfer had just said on the range about yet another player earlier who hit his first shot out of bounds. Even though it was not his own experience, given that his brain was on alert, he then recalled his own worst shot that he had not thought of in years. This is all happening because our brain is searching for context for the threat alert.

It is, therefore, very important for a golfer to take inventory of those past negative experiences so that he or she is, at a bare minimum, aware of what they are and can anticipate the nature of the negative monologues when they occur. In this book, you will learn how to do this as well as how to proactively induce positive monologues during the round, but more importantly, during those unpredictable surprises.

Exercise:
Your Negative Memory Bank

Make a list of the experiences of your life that you feel are possibly stored in your negative memory bank.

1.

2.

3.

4.

5.

Exercise:
Your Negative Monologues

Make a list of the most common negative monologues you have with yourself after a bad shot.

1.

2.

3.

4.

5.

Exercise:
Your Positive Monologues

Make a list of the most common positive monologues you have with yourself when you are in the zone.

1.

2.

3.

4.

5.

"Success depends almost entirely on how effectively you manage the game's two ultimate adversaries: the course and yourself." -Jack Nicklaus

How to Increase your EQ (Theta Waves)

Managing emotions, the *feelings* we have, is the first step to being in a zone. Recall the neurological sequence shown earlier. Emotions dictate thought. Feeling calm and relaxed is an emotional state. This feeling leads to the theta brain waves that are, in fact, waves present when performing in a zone.

Figure 4 shows an actual EKG (electrocardiogram) of just the alpha and theta brain waves. You can see how these waves have frequency.

The fewer the thoughts, the fewer the brain waves. The more negative the thought, the higher the frequency (Hz) of the brain wave. Lower frequency brain waves exist when operating in a zone, the highest state of performance. Having this visual in mind will be key in understanding the GYRA Scorecard as you will be scoring yourself, essentially. The waves below, alpha and theta, are associated with the left-brain picture of the brain labeled "Low Cortisol" a few pages earlier. The "low" acknowledging the low frequency of brain waves when in Green mode. Negative thoughts, by definition, are higher frequency brain waves, sometimes well over 30 Hz. These intense frequencies (Hz) lead to the physiological condition shown earlier where performance is compromised. I will teach you how to become your own EKG machine when playing.

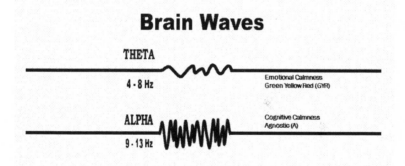

Figure 4. Alpha and Theta "Zone" Brain Waves

The first step in increasing your EQ, your ability to recognize and change your emotion, is to learn to take your emotional temperature. You have to know what you are feeling in order to change it to what you need to feel. Imagine an old thermometer – the kind you stick in your mouth. Imagine there are only three recordings it can give you, GREEN, YELLOW, and RED (GYR), similar to that of a traffic light.

Cortisol

Dopamine

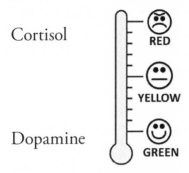

Figure 5. Emotional Thermometer

Green (G) indicates that you are comfortable, happy, stress-free, and can think clearly and perform well. Green means you have low frequency theta waves, which are what allow you to think clearly.

Now that you understand the neuroscience behind Green, you will note that the prefrontal lobes have sent a low threat level signal to the amygdala while in this state. This essentially means your brain, where all of the memories of your golf practice and skills are stored, can easily retrieve those skills, memories, and make good decisions — the centerpiece of your performing at your best. It also means that the negative memories do not have to be accessed, which enhances your chances of being in a zone, since only positive monologues occur here. Green is a good temperature reading. You can learn how to give yourself an accurate reading by referring to the diagram above showing the body's state when in the Red state. When Green, you will naturally feel relaxed, you will feel like all your senses are alert, you will naturally have positive monologues and recall positive experiences, you will remember all of your focal thoughts in all the parts of the game of golf, and you will feel like nothing can throw you off your game.

Yellow (Y) temperature reading indicates that you are a little stressed and anxious. Something has gone wrong in the round, but it is not fatal. The wind picked up during your shot, or you hit a shot slightly left when you meant to hit it straight, or your ball landed in a divot – the list goes on and on of things that can go wrong that can take us off Green to Yellow. You are not in Green for sure because everything just described in Green is not happening, but you are also not in Red where the consequences are very serious. In Yellow, negative dialogues are occurring, but you are able to recollect some positive ones, too. It is an internal battle. For most golfers, golf is played in this state. For context, 4 out 5 Americans are permanently in a state of Yellow in life. If you believe sports reflect life, then it should be no surprise that golf is mostly played in Yellow. This color label is a new language that describes all things we have discussed thus far regarding the brain.

Red (R) is when you are implicitly or explicitly out of control, filled with anger and rage, or disappointment and frustration. You are filled with negative monologues, even being abusive to yourself and perhaps others around you like your caddie or volunteers. You are looking to blame someone instead of finding a solution. You are frustrated that you cannot think clearly or remember much. This happens when the perceived threat is interpreted in your brain as fatal. At this point, you feel missing your goal is imminent and very likely. The sheer volume of thoughts and brain waves is enormous, and so is their intensity. It is the farthest point from being in the zone.

"When you're playing poorly, you start thinking too much. That's when you confuse yourself." –Greg Norman

| Green | Yellow | Red |

Figure 6. Brain Scan When Emotionally Green, Yellow, Red

Brain scan technology has evolved to where we can measure and see visually brain activity during each of these three emotional temperatures. The figure above illustrates the scan of each one. Brain waves carry a current at a certain frequency. The more the brain waves, the higher the "heat" of the current. You can see here that a Green brain scan looks like a large field of little intensity. This brain is optimistic. It will find the right positive narrative after any situation. If the ball ends in a bad lie, this brain will have a confident "I've got this" response naturally.

A Yellow brain scan shows patches of heat (negative thoughts) and a few Red spots depending on what the stimulus was. In the Red brain scan, you can barely see any clear area. The ability to be rational, to make good decisions, and get the physical body to do what you want it to do are all compromised. These Yellow and Red brains become more pessimistic because they are processing high intensity negative memories. If the ball ends up in a bad lie, Yellow and Red brains will find people to blame, excuses to make, and negative memories to recall. Unintentional but instinctive cursing or club-throwing can occur.

If you compare this picture to your golf clubs, perhaps it will be clearer. Green means your clubs are clean with no damage. Yellow could mean that your clubs are dirty, have mud on them, or the grips are not good. You are now gambling with your shot. Red means you have completely damaged clubs. The lie, loft, and shaft flex on each club has been compromised. You have brought pure luck into whether or not you will hit a good shot. Your brain is a "club" you use on every shot. The same odds apply if your brain is Yellow or Red.

This is a new language you are now learning to use in golf, GYR – Green, Yellow, and Red – to identify how your body is at any given point of the round. You can see now why it is so important to know your EQ temperature during the round. The good news is that taking your emotional temperature is not something you can only practice in a round or during practice. Remember how all decisions are made – not just golf ones? Everything starts with emotions, in and out of golf. So, no matter where you are or what you are doing, every three hours of a normal day, starting today, take your emotional temperature and give yourself a color reading. Are you Green, Yellow, or Red? After about a week of this, start to do it more often, perhaps every hour and then start to do it during practice and the round.

In the GYRA Scorecard, we will keep score of GYR per hole. Just like you keep score against par per hole, GYRA will require you to keep score of your emotional state (temperature) after each hole. It is knowing where you are before each hole starts that will allow you to make the necessary adjustment to get to Green. If you are Green, you will be able to retrieve the right memories, skills, and context to play the hole. **This is the first test of golf, not the shot you are about to hit.**

As stated earlier, *the most difficult shot in golf is the one right after a bad one.* Now you know why. After a bad shot, without any active action from you, you are sure to retrieve other negative memories, disable your brain, and compromise your decision-making ability. You are either Yellow or Red after a bad shot. For this reason, this shot is the most difficult one because you are now in an internal war between your conscious and subconscious brain. Your body, your equipment, has changed. Getting your body out of Yellow or Red and back to Green is EQ. It is a different intelligence and skill. How to do this before you get to the next shot or hole will be described in detail later.

You must become a master at taking your own temperature. You do not have a coach or team member out there during the round (unless you have a caddie who is a psychologist) who can help you do this. Clearly, if you are Green, then nothing needs to be done mentally or emotionally. Just keep going and maintain your focus. But if you are Yellow or Red, in that 93% of time, then something has to happen to get you back to Green as fast as possible.

If Jack Nicklaus said he only hit one shot a round that was perfect, then consider for yourself that at least 60 other shots are going to put you, whether you are consciously aware of it or not, in Yellow or Red. Research has shown that it is rare to go from Green directly to Red unless something very dramatic happens. Usually, we progress slowly into Yellow without being aware of it, and stay in Yellow for a while, at which point, nothing dramatic is required to elevate to Red because you are essentially a fuse just waiting to be lit. This is another common mistake many professional golfers make. They do not do enough when in Yellow to get back to Green, and often think they are mentally strong to go from Red directly back to Green. This can be done, but it is much harder.

To state the obvious, the goal is to stay in Green (theta waves) as much as possible. Note that this is an emotional state that leads to a brain state. Chapters 4 through 8 will discuss very specific surprise situations, emotional and mental, to help with typical scenarios in all aspects of golf: practice, pre-round, round, and post-round. In this chapter, by establishing these Green, Yellow, and Red standards, you now have a language you can use with your friends and coaches to help you prepare in a customized manner, one that is unique to your own brain software.

Becoming an Emotional Accountant

Once you have learned how to take your EQ temperature, then and only then can you know how to regulate yourself back to Green. The things you would do to go from Yellow back to Green are very different from the things you would do to go from Red back to Green. Not every surprise is a Red. Emotionally, missing a 40-foot putt is very different from missing a one-foot putt. Missing the one-foot putt is much more emotionally expensive. This is emotional accounting.

As a scenario to further illustrate this point, imagine two golfers playing together, Mark and Tyler. This first hole is a par-five. Mark hits a great drive in the middle of the fairway. Tyler hits a very poor shot into the woods and is forced to punch out. Mark hits an incredible second shot just barely off the green. Tyler hits his third shot into the greenside bunker. Mark chooses to chip and the ball looks like it is going in, but instead hits the pin and is about three feet away. Tyler hits another poor bunker shot to about 15 feet, but makes the putt for par. Mark has to wait and watch Tyler's par putt go in. Mark's subconscious is telling him that "Tyler is so lucky," but he goes through his routine. Mark missed the putt and taps in for par.

Even though both players wrote down 5 on their golf score card, the emotional cost to each one of them could not be more different. The emotional state and therefore, brain waves, for each player going to the second hole was different with identical scores. You can imagine Tyler feeling like it was an all-world par and was feeling Green. Mark was likely feeling Red, not just because he hit perfect shots, missed a 3-footer for birdie, but because it did not seem fair that Tyler was all over the place and they both had the same score. Their brains were retrieving different memories as they walked to the second hole, almost entirely subconsciously (taking the subconscious level to above 90%), and concurrently increasing mind wandering to also well above the 65% average as all kinds of past or future scenarios began to play out. Each of them has unique software (brain memories) that determines the extent of the Yellow/Red state. Mark may have recalled the day before when he made birdie on the same hole, for example, and how good it felt to start that way, but how different it feels now. Tyler's subconscious took him to a place of excitement for a great par or a sense of exhaustion because he had been fighting to save pars a lot lately.

Whatever the cost is, you can now see just how critical it is in golf to be able to capture the Emotional Score (GYR) after each hole using your own EQ Thermometer. Because the software for both Mark and Tyler are different, what each one will have to do to get back to Green will also be different.

One of the challenges of my job as a neuroscientist is to make all the emerging and complex research simple to understand. Over 10 years ago, I created the Green-Yellow-Red emotional temperature label, and published it in my blogs and previous books, because I wanted a universal language. Green-Yellow-Red is on every traffic light in the world, irrespective of language, and there is a traffic light in every country in the world. Green means go, Red means stop, and Yellow means caution in the traffic light colors. This is already understood and should make your own adaption of using these colors for emotions easier.

Even in other sports, a Red card, for example in soccer or lacrosse, is a severe penalty. A Yellow card is also a penalty, but less severe. Using these colors as new labels for emotions is critical to properly self-diagnosing yourselves. Traditional labels like happy, sad, mad, glad, angry, upset, frustrated, and such, are vague and subjective, and they come with a stigma that often results in being defensive. Colors are innocuous by contrast, do not have a stigma, do not conjure defense mechanisms, and accurately reflect what is actually happening to your brain.

In order to practice using these colors, self-awareness of emotions is going to be a skill you will have to master. Figure 7 shows a speedometer model of the EQ Thermometer. As suggested earlier, imagine that this speedometer is invisible over your head at all times, but especially during your round. Imagine where the needle is pointing at the end of each hole, a sum total of everything that happened on the hole you just finished. Off the course, you can practice this by asking yourself where the needle is pointing on the speedometer and truthfully answering that question, say, every 1-2 hours. During your round of golf, you will need to do this after each hole so that you know exactly what to do to move that needle towards Green.

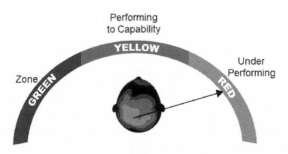

Figure 7. Emotional Speedometer

The GYR part of the GYRA Scorecard

Figure 8 below is your first glimpse into the GYRA Mental Scorecard. It is part of the process where you can become your own EKG machine, giving you power to know exactly where your emotions and thoughts are. This will be the first step, to know what to change in you, how to change it, and how much of it to change to get those brain waves back to alpha and theta level. Note:

1. Your emotional temperature is captured on the same traditional golf scorecard.

2. One single row for each emotional temperature is designated. There should be three separate rows, one for Green on top, Yellow in the middle, and Red at the bottom.

3. You will put an "X" after each hole on the specific golf hole as to what you feel your emotional temperature is based on the cost of all the shots on the hole you just finished. Therefore, you will enter an X 18 times, one per hole, going from left, hole number 1, to right, finishing on hole 18.

4. At the end of the round, this self-reporting emotional scan, like an actual EKG reading, will reflect how well you were able to manage yourself emotionally, and how well you were able to achieve theta waves.

5. Just like we keep golf score against par, we will keep GYR against Green. Theta waves occur when you are Green. This should be considered Birdie or better. Yellow should be considered par and Red should be considered bogey or worse. This is an emotional score being suggested, not a golf score, so you can have a comparable measurement to golf, to make it easier to understand.

6. It is critical to note that your actual golf score and GYR "X" score may be not be the same. I will discuss this below*.

7. The scorecard shown in Figure 9 is incomplete. It is missing the A in the GYRA. The A, agnostic measurement, will be discussed in the next chapter.

8. There are two GYRA scorecards below. The first is what it should look like before your round (blank). The second is what it should look like after your round (GYR completed).

HOLE	1	2	3	4	5	6	7	8	9	OUT	10	11	12	13	14	15	16	17	18	IN	TOTAL
YARDAGE	436	176	451	608	213	410	595	192	452	3533	431	564	239	382	439	180	381	661	460	3737	7270
PAR	4	3	4	5	3	4	5	3	4	35	4	5	3	4	4	3	4	5	4	36	71
YOUR SCORE																					
G																					
Y																					
R																					
A																					

Figure 8. GYRA Scorecard: Blank

Figure 8 shows a blank GYRA Scorecard that can be created using any golf scorecard at any course. Instead of putting names of people in the empty rows, just insert GYRA per row.

To illustrate point number 6 above* and show that emotional temperature and actual golf score (against par) may not be the same, a golfer could hit two spectacular shots on a par-four with his approach shot just three feet from the hole. Consider him missing that putt and making par. The golf score is par, but the emotional temperature could be Yellow or even Red, depending on the person, the hole it occurred on, what another player in the group did, and what that missed putt meant to the overall score.

For a golfer who has made five birdies in a row, missing that putt would likely be of no emotional cost because so much positive deposits were made to dilute the impact of the missed shot on the brain and body. Conversely, for a golfer who has made five bogeys, is already in Yellow or Red and finally has a chance to get one back, and misses a three-footer, being Red is the likely GYR score.

Because this is self-reporting, it is of the highest importance that the golfer be honest. It is of no value to lie to yourself. Golfers are not going to share their GYRA Scorecards with each other. Keeping actual golf score itself is self-reporting and based on the powerful honor code in the game of golf. Arguably, lying on your golf scorecard, cheating, is considered almost an unrecoverable sin and a DQ. The same honor should be extended to keeping your emotional GYR score. If you give yourself an incorrect reading, you will likely make the wrong adjustment. An incorrect self-assessment is essentially DQing yourself from a true learning and improvement experience. We will come back to this later when we put the GYRA card together with the Agnostic scores.

Once you take your GYR score on each hole, you have time before you get to the next tee box. The time clearly depends on the physical distance between finished green and next tee box, on how long you have to wait for your partners to finish a hole before going to next tee box, and on when it is your turn to hit on the next box. However long it is, this time should be viewed similar to a coach's timeout in other sports, where a coach calls a timeout to regroup and make adjustments. Golfers are fortunate to have these natural timeouts between holes to assess the cumulative cost of the finished hole.

Once you put an X on the finished hole, right after you putt out the hole, depending on your reading, it is then time to make adjustments. If your temperature is Green, which is rare, then a conscious effort to stay Green is key. If a baseball pitcher has a no hitter going, his teammates sit away from him so as not to cause any distraction. If your temperature is Yellow, which is more often, then the adjustment to make is different than if your temperature is Red.

Figure 9 shows a completed GYRA Scorecard, but with the Agnostic row empty for now. We will complete this row in the next chapter. It is an actual scorecard kept by an LPGA player during a tournament. Note the yardages are from the normal course golf scorecard which she got from the pro shop to use as her GYRA card, but actual yardages per hole were much less. I did not have the yardages she actually played because it was on her scoring card which she had to turn in. But the yardages are irrelevant to the GYRA process.

HOLE	1	2	3	4	5	6	7	8	9	OUT	10	11	12	13	14	15	16	17	18	IN	TOTAL
YARDAGE	436	178	451	608	213	410	595	192	452	3533	431	564	239	382	439	190	381	661	460	3737	7270
PAR	4	3	4	5	3	4	5	3	4	35	4	5	3	4	4	3	4	5	4	36	71
ACTUAL SCORE	[5]	3	4	4	(2)	(3)	5	3	(3)	32	4	(4)	3	(3)	(3)	[4]	(3)	5	[5]	34	
G			x	x	x							x	x	x							
Y		x	x			x					x	x				x	x	x	x		
R	x						x	x													
A																					

Figure 9. GYRA Scorecard: GYR Completed

After the round is over, you can see in the next scorecard image that, if you draw a line connecting all the X's across 18 holes, an EKG-type reading of the emotional changes occurs over the course of about five hours. **If you are honest, it will be stunningly close to an actual EKG reading and begin to give you a true account of where your brain is per hole**. In many simulations my team and I conducted, we found close-enough correlations between an honest self-reported GYR score reading and actual theta waves reading. All the brain waves in Red were more in quantity and intensity (above 30 Hz!). Yellow were not too far behind and Green were low, closer to theta waves. More importantly, based on this assessment, where this can really be a game-changer, is that your simple honesty could be good enough to mimic an electronic device, allowing you to make the right adjustments. In Chapters 9 and 10, you will read about how this was taken and used by an LPGA player and the KFT Tour player during competition. The key take-away should be just how simple this can be to use without any wearable or other device.

We will process this same score card in full later so you understand how she gave herself these GYR scores. Worth noting, she did not have her 'A' game on this day, and never felt she was truly in the zone for the majority of the day. However, she made constant adjustments per hole (discussed in Chapter 9) and still managed a 66!

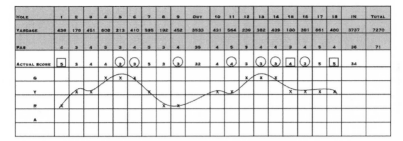

Figure 10. GYRA Scorecard: GYR-EKG

Changing Your Emotional Temperature – GREEN TO GREEN

Now that you know how to take your emotional temperature and label it using one of three colors, let us turn the focus to moving the needle to the left towards Green.

Our five senses are the only connection (entry points) our body has with ever-changing stimuli during golf. Before every shot, as you take your EQ temperature during a round, and you are Green, then the goal is to stay Green proactively. When already in Green, the best way to stay in Green is to actively overuse your five senses. This is called macro- and micro-focus, and will be discussed in further detail in Chapter 4.

You would be using your eyes, for example, to focus your *sight* on the smallest detail of whatever is in front of you. It might be dimples on the ball, or a blade of grass as a target, or the trees on the course, or specific colors on flowers. For *feel*, you would not just be feeling for the wind, but the air around you at every hole and even the air coming in and out of your lungs. Or even feel the energy transfer from your arms to the club and ball, or the sense of your hands on gripping your club or the ground as you walk. For *sound*, it would not be just listening to cheers from volunteers or playing partners, but also to the wind or birds or other sounds you normally would ignore. For *taste*, it can be allowing a sip of water or drink to sit in your mouth for a few seconds longer than normal or doing the same thing with any food. Similarly, for *smell*, it can be focusing on the aroma of the food you are eating or coming from the stands, or sniffing the air around you on the course and catching the scents off the greenery.

Actively engaging the senses is a powerful technique to engage the low frequency alpha and theta waves, and to keep your self-awareness at a high state of alert, an attribute of being in the zone. Since you are consciously doing it, you are reducing the subconscious percentage of your brain activity. If you are this focused and you notice that suddenly, for whatever reason you are *not focused*, then you know your emotional temperature has changed. Something has caused you to lose focus. **It is hard to know you have lost focus if you never had it in the first place**.

I discuss focus and how to use it in greater detail in both practice and rounds in Chapter 4. For now, learn to appreciate your five senses as a critical tool set for staying in the zone, for lower mind wandering, and lower subconscious activity.

"For me, winning isn't something that happens suddenly on the field when the whistle blows and the crowds roar. Winning is something that builds physically and mentally every day that you train and every night that you dream." -Emmitt Smith

Changing Your Emotional Temperature – YELLOW TO GREEN

You have taken your EQ temperature and it is Yellow. The needle on the EQ Speedometer is somewhere in the middle range. This is a sign that you are merely performing, but not in a high performing state. The possibility of unintended poor shots has increased.

The absolute first thing to do when you take your EQ temperature and you are in Yellow is to breathe. This might surprise you since you are probably thinking that you are always breathing – what is up with that? No. Change your breathing. Take a count (cadence) of how long it takes you to breathe in, and take another count of how long it takes you to breathe out in the same normal breath. For most people, this normal breathing count is anywhere from two to five counts breathing in and two to five counts breathing out.

Using the same cadence, practice right now and increase your breath count in to average about 25 and your breath count out to average about 25 also. You can do this by simply taking in your breath slower and releasing your breath longer in a very controlled manner. When the body is physiologically in Yellow, recall that one of the symptoms is increased heart rate and increased breath rate. A lot of oxygen is being channeled to other parts of your body in anticipation of having to "jump to avoid the car" or "run from the roar." Slowing your breath by actively counting 25 in and 25 out will slow down your heart rate, even if just a little at first, and will begin to disable the amygdala and enable the brain. Breathing slowly while your heart rate is high is a conscious move on your part, letting the brain know it is not a real threat where your life is in imminent danger.

You will recall it is only in your brain that all your skills reside. You need your memories of skills and what-to-do list to *not* be compromised for the next shot. This kind of EQ breathing allows your brain waves to lower in volume; and *slow*, controlled breathing is consistent with alpha and theta waves. You should sense almost immediately that the needle on the EQ speedometer is moving to the left towards Green.

ACT (Abdomen, Chest, Throat) Breathing Technique

During physical activity, and especially during a round, there are essentially three levels of breathing that occur. The first is breathing at the throat (T) level – air tends not to feel like it goes anywhere deeper than your mouth. This is typically short and fast breaths where the breath-count in and out is less than two. The second is chest (C) level where the breaths are inhaled chest-deep with breath-counts in and out between two and 10. The last is abdomen (A) level, where a long, slow breath in, to the level your lungs feel like they are touching your abdomen is followed by a long, slow breath out.

During a round, most golfers are not thinking of their breath at all and allow it to be at the mercy of whatever happens. High anxiety situations also automatically trigger your body to the T level of breathing. This is instinctive and in response to the higher heart rate, which itself is a response by the body to prepare you for survival.

Unlike cognitive or brain activity, breathing involves a lot of body parts and muscles, and therefore can be controlled even after the initial burst of anxiety to T level breathing. This is the reason why it should always be the first step in managing EQ, because it is one of the easiest things to do. Though A level breathing is quite challenging to maintain during a round, your goal should be to always be breathing at A level during a round, especially in times of challenging conditions (wind, rain, etc.). I also recommend attempting A level breathing when you are Green. As you are practicing or playing, keep track of what level of ACT (Abdomen, Chest, Throat) you are doing and know you can perform best at the A level, so adjust your breathing accordingly. Learning this is key to the neuroplasticity concept of changing your brain, and the waves in them.

After breathing, the next step in changing your temperature from Yellow to Green is to create a Yellow card. This card will change over time, and maybe even several times more, over the course of a season. Let us create your personalized Yellow card first and then I will elaborate on how to use it to change the temperature (after breathing) from Yellow to Green. Answer the five questions below with just three words or less that will instantly take you back emotionally to a very specific point in time and place.

Exercise:
Your Yellow Card

1. When/where was the best round you have ever had?

2. List all your 14 clubs here and describe where you hit the best shot ever with each club.

Driver

3 Wood

_____

_____

3 Iron

4 Iron

5 Iron

6 Iron

7 Iron

8 Iron

9 Iron

PW

Wedge 1

Wedge 2

Putter

3. When/where was the best recovery shot you have hit?

4. When/where was your best first tee shot?

5. When/where was your best warm up to a round?

Transfer these questions and your responses to a Yellow index card (for your pocket when playing) or perhaps onto your iPhone (during practicing) so that it is portable and can be with you when you need it.

Just as negative and threatening experiences have dire consequences to the chemistry of our body as explained earlier, positive experiences have the opposite effect. They can give us confidence by releasing dopamine, the counter hormone to cortisol (stress hormone) and inspire us to perform better. **Research shows that it takes an average of five positive experiences to dilute a comparable negative experience**. In other words, cortisol is more powerful than dopamine. Recall, again, the burnt hand example from earlier versus the nine great things on that day. The problem during practice, and especially during a round, is that we cannot predict when those positive experiences will happen any more than we can predict when the negative ones will occur. This is all sports, the ultimate reality show.

However, we can be certain that it is very unlikely that the positive experiences will conveniently occur immediately as the negative one is happening so that they can counteract each other. For Mark to get to the second tee box, knowing he is in Yellow, five good things must happen to him to dilute his chemical (emotional) state so that he can think his best on the next shot. Where are those five experiences going to come from? Should Mark decide to do nothing and just walk to the second tee box, he is taking a major gamble. He might hit a good shot or he might not. He is at the mercy of his software, his subconscious. To increase his odds, he has to take full advantage of that time between shots. He has to increase his odds in the gamble.

This is where the Yellow card comes in. Some version of those five positive experiences required for dilution can be induced into your brain to redirect the neuropathways. They are impossible to remember during the "heat of competition" of a round as you have so many competing thoughts and priorities with the clock ticking to your next shot, and therefore writing them down before hand is necessary. You will need this list to counteract the cause of what got you into Yellow so you can get back to Green.

After your breathing, when in Yellow, take a look at your Yellow card however you have decided to craft it. It is critical that you write it down for reading as opposed to relying on memory. Forget how it will look like to a competitor – at this point, your biggest competitor is not another person, it is yourself. **Once Mark got to Yellow, Tyler no longer was his primary competitor. Mark's subconscious became his competitor.**

When playing, as you read what is on the card per the situation, try hard to transport yourself emotionally to that great memory and remember what worked so well and what you are capable of doing. If the next shot Mark has to hit on the second tee box is a driver again, or whatever club, and Mark were to look at his Yellow card of the best most-recent drive he hit and emotionally took himself to that situation, then he has proactively inserted a past experience into his brain.

Let us say the drive on Mark's Yellow card was a drive he hit with on the 18th hole of a previous round under pressure. By reading it from his Yellow card, and emotionally taking himself to that point in time, he is using his own positive memory to compete against the subconsciously induced negative memories and monologues of what just happened on the first hole. This process, coupled with A breathing, reduces the volume of brain waves and the intensity of them because it was a huge positive memory that was recollected. This is how to compete with yourself, your true competition.

The breathing and the Yellow card (induced positive counteracting experiences) will impact your prefrontal lobes, diluting the grip of the amygdala, and allow you to do what you need to do to get back to focusing and to Green. The needle should move further to the left towards Green.

If you look closely during televised golf rounds with professionals, you will often see a small photo of someone taped on a golfer's bag or yardage book. Maybe it is a picture of family or a pet or a loved one that has passed away, but looking at it provides inspiration that could carry him or her from Yellow to Green. These pictures or mementos work in the same way as the Yellow card, and used correctly, can bring a golfer's emotions back from Yellow to Green.

Hostage negotiators use this same technique when working with criminals who have taken hostages. They know the situation is Red, the criminal is Red, and so are the hostages. Their first goal is to emotionally *diffuse* the situation to allow rational thought to have a chance. They are trying to get the needle away from Red towards Yellow or Green so some semblance of logic and reasoning can be used. They do not start with logic and reasoning. They start by **changing the emotional temperature**. Sometimes, they will bring in the wife or child of the criminal to talk to them directly. Hearing their voices can be a very powerful dilutor of Red emotions, diffusing the criminal's Red state and allowing for a safe resolution.

When in Yellow or Red, you are your own hostage negotiator as you are being held captive emotionally and cognitively by thousands of years of brain design and your own negative memories. You have to re-write your brain software as you play.

Changing Your Emotional Temperature – RED TO GREEN

The needle on the EQ Speedometer is all the way on the right in the Red. It is a long way from Green and therefore, something much different and much more of a quick and immediate impact has to be done to move the needle left. Even getting to Yellow from Red is better than doing nothing.

When something terrible has occurred and you have taken your emotional temperature and diagnosed yourself as Red, the first step is again to immediately breathe in the same way as the process for Yellow to Green. This will be a little harder, but more important to do. Try your best to get to A Level of breathing. In Red, your breathing will be very intense (T level), your heart rate very high and your vision blurred, just to a mention a few symptoms. Look at Figure 3 again.

The process to go from Red to Green is similar to the Yellow transformation. You need to create a Red card, but the content will be very different. You will still need to induce positive experiences, but they have to be of a very different and very powerful kind.

My first Ironman race as a pro was in 2002 at Ironman Wisconsin. One reason I became a professional was because I wanted to do the Wisconsin race as that was near my hometown of Sussex. I spent the year training, going to Madison and working on the course, and was very confident going into it. I attended the press conference, which I was not invited to, but still went and listened. No one knew who I was. Listening to the pro women, I still had belief in myself and that I could win.

I registered and received my lucky number 33 and thought I was all ready. During the race I had a fabulous initial win. I saw the top pro ahead of me and passed her on the bike with all media camera on me now! I had a phenomenal bike ride, but when I got off the bike my legs hurt so badly that I couldn't run. I ran anyway but couldn't keep up, started walking and got passed.

Half way, on the sidelines I saw my daughter and mother-in-law, both in their wheelchairs, screaming for me, and I thought how awful that I was feeling sorry for myself for having aching legs. They would have given anything to walk just a mile. I ran over, gave them a hug and a high five, and started running again with only their faces on my mind, and won the Ironman.

-Heather Gollnick, Five-Time Ironman Champion

Though Heather's story above has nothing to do with golf, it is very powerful and clearly was incredibly effective to get her from almost not finishing at the half way mark of the run to winning the Ironman in 2002, and underscores just how powerful emotions can be. The visual stimuli of seeing her daughter and mother-in-law in wheelchairs moved that needle so powerfully that it did not just move to Yellow, but all the way to Green, and led to her winning the Ironman in a come-from-behind fashion.

Stories like this are not new in sports, but they have never been studied in a way that can be duplicated at the right time of competition. The same applies to golf. You, however, may not have your daughter and mother-in-law in a wheelchair in your round, and do not need to, to orchestrate a similar transformation in your brain during a Red state situation. You can self-induce similarly powerful experiences by completing the Red card below. The Red card, unlike the Yellow one, rarely changes and is used in those rare Red situations we all hope not to have.

Your personalized Red card: Answer the five questions below with just three words or less that will instantly take you back to that point in memory, time, and place.

Exercise:
Your Red Card

1. What are the first names of the most important people in your life?

2. What are the first names of your best friends – the ones that will be your friends for life?

3. When/where was the place you have been happiest in your life?

4. Who is the person, dead or alive, that you aspire to be like off the golf course and why?

5. What are you most proud of in your life – an accomplishment not given to you that no one else can ever take from you?

In addition to this card being in your yardage book similar to the Yellow card instructions, you may also wish to have pictures or mementos that can have a similar impact. One tour player carries a rock from the grave of the most important person in her life. When she is Red, she takes it out of her bag and looks at it. She has told me she can sense the shift in her brain as she consciously shifts her neuropathways from what she did with a golf ball to someone she would love to have just one more conversation with.

The Yellow and Red experiences are *your* positive experiences and one of the more under-utilized assets you have. You know your brain will neurologically attract *your* negative memories when in Yellow or Red. It is designed to do so. Your job is to attract positive ones at the right time, after a bad shot, between shots, so that you can make the best decision for the next shot and allow your physical body to do what you have trained it to do, and what you *know* you are capable of doing.

To repeat, the first step in properly recording the GYR part of the GYRA Scorecard is to become very good at taking your emotional temperature. In order to practice using these colors, self-awareness of emotions is a skill you will have to master. Imagining that invisible EQ speedometer over your head and truthfully seeing where the needle is pointing is a simple way to do this. It is something you can also easily practice off the course. If you have a caddie, teammate, coach, or parent, you can ask them to look at you and guess where your EQ temperature is. Do not be surprised if the temperature reading you give yourself is different from what they give you. Be open to the findings I discovered, which is that others' readings of you are often more accurate than your reading of yourself. This collaboration can be valuable in you becoming better at assessing yourself in the heat of competition. You will find an obvious correlation between your temperature and the quality of the decisions and shots you are making.

In the next chapters, I will teach you additional ways to make adjustments and have an actual framework for the entire round. In this chapter, you were introduced to a new emotional language, GYR, and two neuroplasticity-based GYRA tools (ACT breathing and Cards) to help you get to Green. These are just two of 14 others we will discuss. In the next chapter, we will shift from managing emotions to managing thoughts.

Now, let's redefine emotional strength:

Emotional strength is the accurate recognition of your emotional temperature. You know about the EQ Speedometer.

Emotional strength is recognition that if Yellow or Red, your brain and neuromuscular body will underperform. You know you can move the needle.

Emotional strength is taking steps to go from Yellow or Red to Green. You know how to move the needle towards Green no matter the temperature.

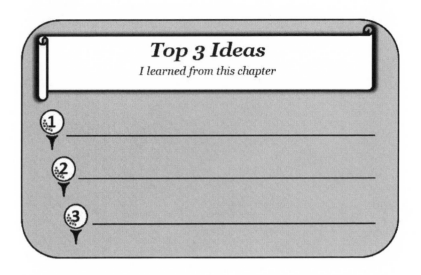

Top 3 Ideas

I learned from this chapter

1. _____

2. _____

3. _____

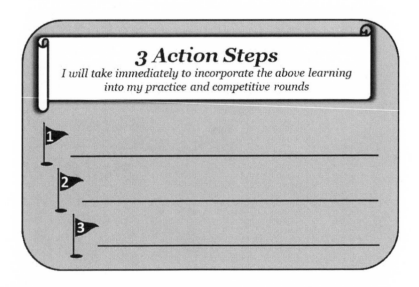

3 Action Steps

I will take immediately to incorporate the above learning into my practice and competitive rounds

1. _____

2. _____

3. _____

Chapter Summary

1. Your goal must be to perform at your best during the round that matters. This means making good decisions.

2. The physiological sequence of making good decisions starts with our emotions, not our skills or thinking. Therefore, understanding emotions is critical to optimal performance, to playing in the zone.

3. All our golf skills are stored in our brain, and in no other part of our body. The brain can be shut off as an instinctive survival response to any danger, perceived or real. When the brain is disabled, poor decisions are made.

4. Knowing your emotional temperature at all times of the round is critical to your performance. There are three EQ Temperature readings – Green, Yellow, and Red.

5. Alpha and theta brain waves, the ones present when playing in the zone, are associated with a Green emotional temperature.

6. Negative thoughts, occurring in Yellow and Red emotional conditions, are more in quantity and higher in frequency, resulting in physiological changes to the body, any of which will compromise any golf skill you have.

7. The GYRA Scorecard is a way to self-assess your brain as you play each hole, creating a real-time EKG-type reading for each round.

8. It takes an average of five positive memories to dilute one negative one. When playing golf, we can pre-plan these positive memories in cards and induce them into the conscious brain to process and reduce cortisol levels.

9. The cards, Yellow or Red, and the ACT breathing model are two of many GYRA tools to use to change the EKG-reading before going to the next hole.

10. These techniques begin to lay the foundation of being a golfer with a high EQ.

Chapter 4

- *You would never accept a laptop from someone saying, "It only works great when the weather is great, it's feeling good, and has rested/exercised/eaten well," - yet that is what we do with our brains, ourselves, and others.*
- *We don't make time to enjoy our past positive experiences ... a life delicacy usually enjoyed late in life ... yet a daily dose of it is a powerful neurological nutrient for mental health.*
- *If your good friend was sad/negative in demeanor, would that be the right time for you to ask for advice from him? Or would you first try to make them happy, and then ask? The same logic applies to you!! You cannot make good decisions in competition being sad /sulky and the clock is ticking! You will give yourself bad advice, and you'll take that bad advice!*

@izzyjustice

Agnostic (A)

Traveling light

In the GYRA Model of keeping a mental scorecard, we have learned about the GYR. These are emotions that precede thought. These emotions constitute mostly the theta waves dominant in being in a zone of performance. Alpha waves are also dominant and this is largely the state of being in the present moment, not in the past or the future, what we are calling being Agnostic. A good metaphor for thoughts, just like the speedometer for emotions, is traveling light. If you travel with a lot of luggage, bags of clothes and stuff perhaps, it is hard to travel far without getting tired. The more thoughts in your brain, the harder it is for alpha waves to occur. More thoughts mean more waves, higher frequency waves, and limited ability for the brain to process the neuromuscular task at hand. Traveling lightly mentally is a good thought to keep when thinking of alpha waves.

Remember, muscles have no memory. The brain is the commander-in-chief. A signal has to be sent from the brain to muscles to hit a driver, hit an iron, or hit a putt. These are all performed by your muscles. For the purpose of illustration only, if I were to cut the "wire" between your brain and muscles, with both your brain and muscles functioning by themselves perfectly, no signals would travel to your muscles and your muscles would just sit there waiting for a command. This is what being a quadriplegic is.

Figure 11 depicts an image of those "wires" from the brain to muscles. It is what we call the nervous system. Everything that we are, our hopes, dreams, emotions, thoughts, and actions, are conducted through this system of the brain and its "cable system." Brain waves travel from the brain via these nerves to the muscles. The higher frequency brain waves (negative) tend to compromise the sequence of body movement (swing) and sense of force (speed). We will discuss this more later. Bottom line – we underperform because the transportation system to carry a skill (from the brain) to the muscle is in a different frequency than what you trained that skill in. **Luggage is much heavier through these nerves when there are too many thoughts and/or thoughts have a higher frequency.** When you are on the range or playing a casual round, I am guessing like most, you play much better than when in competition. This is because the brain waves on the range and casual rounds are fewer and lower frequency, traveling light, and signals from the brain to the muscles through the cable system (nerves) are transported without issues. In competitive rounds, there are infinitely more stimuli for the brain to process, naturally creating more (quantity) brain waves and, regrettably, increased higher frequency (negative) ones, too.

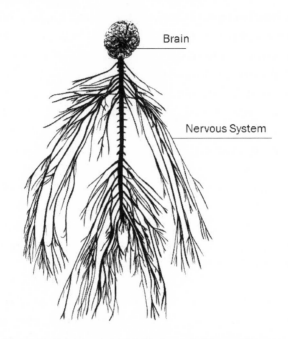

Figure 11. Brain and the "Cable System" (Nervous System)

If you are on the 17th hole and realize that you need to par to win a tournament, shoot 65, break par or shoot your best round, these unsolicited thoughts are not Agnostic. On the same hole, if you think about the water on the left, the last hole where you missed a putt, or mis-hit a wedge, or the last time you were in this situation and you either performed well or did not, these unsolicited thoughts are not Agnostics either. All these thoughts occurred at a different point in time than the present moment, but are played in your brain, similar to an actual person standing next to you talking to you while you are trying to swing. As I noted earlier, you would be furious at that person, and if you hit a poor shot, you would justifiably blame that person because it is clear that the talking somehow compromised the signals from your brain to your muscles, altering what you intended to do versus what happened. This same simple logic applies to those non-agnostics that our own brain is playing during our pre-shot routine or swing.

The holy grail of mental strength (as opposed to emotional) is to be Agnostic over each shot. In that agnostic moment, you are nowhere in the world except in that specific moment in time, in that specific geo-spatial point in the geography of the world. Because of this, the signal from brain to muscle is light, not burdened with past or future narratives. It feels like all your senses are fully activated, and your sense of conscious power (as opposed to subconscious) is very high as you feel like you can make the ball do exactly what you intend to do. Mind wandering is extremely low when Agnostic. This is identical to the crowd or playing partners being quiet as you hit the ball. Why are they quiet when you are hitting a shot? Because we all know already, intuitively, without being a neuroscientist, that if everyone is not quiet, our brain is distracted, has to process all the crowd stimuli, and it is really hard to hit a good shot.

There is a test I do when I coach golfers, especially from good golfers to professional golfers. I always go play at least nine holes with them. After each shot is hit, I ask them what they were thinking before the shot or over the shot. I can trace every bad shot to first of all being not agnostic. In one instance, a pro hit a poor chip shot. It was a stock shot, nothing much to it really. I asked him what he was thinking. He first said, "Not sure." I pushed harder for an answer, and he then said, "I think I was thinking of hitting the ball." I pushed even harder and told him to be honest with me. He then said, "You know what, just before I hit the shot, I think I said to myself that the greens were slow today." This subconscious non-agnostic thought interfered with a very low physical effort shot where the signal from brain to muscle was compromised. **The difference between a playing partner or fan talking during your backswing versus your own brain talking during your backswing is only that the former is much clearer to identify.** The effect is the same.

When Mark and Tyler left the first hole, although they were playing by themselves, their monologues during their walk to the second tee box were actually like four or five people following each one, every one of them saying something different to them, and at least three of the people were being quite negative about what happened. If this actually happened, both Mark and Tyler would probably ask them to shut up and allow them to go play. But when both Mark and Tyler were doing it to themselves, they had no framework to process those monologues to tell themselves to shut up. In all their hours of practice on the range and short game areas, this is not something they practiced at all. They did not even know how to practice for it. Why would they be good at it?

A non-agnostic thought is an actual neuropathway, a set of brain waves usually of a negative nature, that competes with the same current as an alpha current. Remember, an alpha current is a low frequency current of 9-13 Hz. It is no match for the higher frequency current of negative thoughts. This, in turn, will compromise the signal from your brain to muscles resulting in hitting a shot not as you intended.

You can do that exercise yourself. When you hit a poor shot, force yourself to diagnose what the non-agnostic thought was. You, too, will quickly be able to realize that any thought about the future or past not relevant to the shot at hand, will likely be the culprit of the poor shot.

What is very interesting is that after the poor shot, the pro rehearsed several chips, subconsciously shifting the focus to a technique issue instead of a mental issue. In working with golfers around the world at all levels, **I find that the most prevalent mistake made is identifying the wrong problem**, and then wasting time, hard work, and money fixing the wrong problem. You must be convinced that if you have the skill to hit a particular shot, and you have done it on command several times before, whether on the range or in competition, then when you cannot pull off that same shot in competition, it is not a technique issue. The first step cannot be to go see your instructor or to change your equipment, your grip, or whatever. However, if there is a consistency to your mistakes and they are happening on the range and in competition, then yes, it is likely time to see your instructor.

In golf, there are only four types of shot results:

1. Good Shot Good Result (GSGR)
2. Good Shot Bad Result (GSBR)
3. Bad Shot Bad Result (BSBR)
4. Bad Shot Good Result (BSGR)

It is worth taking the time to process each of these.

Good Shot Good Result (GSGR)

If you hit a shot exactly how you intended to, and the result was also exactly as you intended, this is a GSGR. This is the *only* measure you should use to determine whether you were fully agnostic. This is a "dot" on the card, as will be described later. This means you processed all the variables (lie, wind, distance, trajectory, club, etc.) correctly.

From an emotional cost perspective, this is actually a deposit, not an accounting withdrawal. Proverbially, this can be considered "a shot in the arm," or "momentum," as your brain processes this result in a positive and empowering manner. Dopamine is secreted and this has a diluting impact on previous bad shots. Being Green and Agnostic after this is much easier. Keep in mind that one good shot and one bad shot are not of equal emotional and cognitive cost. As a rule of thumb, it will take about five GSGRs to dilute any one of the shots below.

Good Shot Bad Result (GSBR)

If you hit a shot exactly as you intended, thinking you had done a great job processing all the variables, and the result was not good, the surprise was very high on the result, this is GSBR. Clearly, you missed something in the decision-making process. Mind wandering is very high as a result because of the high surprise factor. **In the hundreds of interviews we conducted, and associated brain scans, we found – surprisingly – that this shot is by far the most expensive one emotionally and cognitively.** Much more expensive than the two other shots below. It is a massive release of cortisol in the body, tension is very high as heart rate and blood flow quickly changes (see Figure 3), **resulting in a startling discovery: the 2 shots (BSGR and BSBR) below occur mostly after this shot, GSBR.** The surprise of the result is highest in this shot, making it much longer for the brain to be fully ready and much less agnostic before the next shot. As a golfer, knowing this can be a huge indicator to do something before the next shot, otherwise a poor shot is likely to occur.

Bad Shot Bad Result (BSBR)

This is a shot where you hit it not as you intended and the result was also not as you intended. We found that even though these shots are costly both in golf score and emotionally/cognitively, they are not nearly as costly as GSBR. We learned that this is largely because the golfer was able to identify the cause, unlike in the GSBR scenario. This ability to identify the cause reduced mind wandering and the surprise result for the brain. The larger the surprise, the more activated the subconscious. This shot is costly nonetheless, and adjustments have to be made before the next shot.

Bad Shot Good Result (BSGR)

This is when you hit a poor shot but the result turned out good. It is costly also, but not from a golf perspective, only from an emotional and cognitive one. The cost is relatively low because the good result dilutes the surprise factor, and the visual stimulus of the good result allows the brain to quickly transition to the next shot.

You can see how each one of these results has a different cognitive cost, very similar to how Mark and Tyler played their first hole and how, emotionally, the cost of that hole was different to each one even though they both had the same score. **The cognitive luggage created with each shot result IS to be carried by the brain to the next shot.** An adjustment better be made or the probability of a next good shot will be lowered.

Note that these findings are based on my research. Using scientific methods, my team analyzed exactly 500 GYRA Scorecards over a 12-month period. Male and female golfers of all levels from juniors to tour professionals filled the cards out per shot and per hole in one-day, two-day, three-day and four-day tournaments. The randomized methods included interviews with golfers that completed them, transferring the scorecards to a database that allowed us to analyze and find causations and correlations between the type of shot results and the subsequent shots, and the golf score on each hole and on preceding holes. You know how the GYR (emotions) is scored and I will show you how to be your own EKG machine with being Agnostic (A) later.

Surprises

The brain does not like surprises. Period. In competition, surprises are very expensive cognitively. Surprises are heavy luggage. Having surprises in your brain is not traveling light. For our purposes, the definition of a surprise is simple: **something you did not expect.** The surprise could be either something good or something bad, but in both cases, you did not expect it. A surprise is like a grenade for the subconscious. When presented with a surprise, the brain tries to make sense of it. It is designed to do just that.

Think of our cavemen ancestors who, during a hunt, suddenly see a pack of lions coming at them. Panic sets in largely because their brain is sent into a tailspin trying to figure out where they came from, how they did not hear or see them earlier, what steps to take to get away or to fight them, and so on. There is a lot to process in the brain after a surprise. When the surprise is in competition, in golf, the brain suspends much of its conscious brain in order to figure out the surprise while at the same time having to physically keep moving and knowing there is an imminent next shot to hit.

The hardware of our brain is still very much like our cavemen friends. A surprise is a gift to mind wandering as the brain now tries to do many things at the same time. A negative surprise is the most expensive one cognitively because you did not intend for it, and the impact/consequence of it could be severe as golf is a cumulative score; every shot counts towards the score. In most ball sports, mis-hitting a shot is not as costly as it is in golf. In soccer, if you attempt to pass the ball and the opposing team steals it, it is rare that the mis-hit costs you a goal. In tennis, you can lose a set 0-6, but still win the remaining sets and win the match. In stroke play golf, every shot has the measurable cost of a stroke. A shot hit out of bounds or a missed two-foot putt will add to the final score. **Make no mistake, your subconscious brain is fully aware of this**.

The impact of a surprise to the brain, the waves in it, the intensity of the frequency, mind wandering, and subconscious are all very dire. Again, this is not traveling light! But not all surprises are the same. Luggage can all weigh different. If there was a tail wind and you took less club to adjust and in mid-flight the wind died and the ball came just short of the pin, and still having a birdie, yes it was a surprise that the wind changed, but not a big one. In the same scenario, if you took enough club to cover the front of the green no matter the tail wind and came up a full club short with the ball in the hazard, well that is a huge surprise. The latter will have more of an impact on the brain than missing your spot by a few feet. If you are aiming at the middle of the fairway for a T shot, push the shot a little and it ends on the right side of the fairway. It is a surprise, but one your brain will not go into a subconscious tailspin for as it is likely not going to try to figure out what happened, who to blame, and how to fix the problem. If you hit a perfect putt thinking you could make it but it ends up going 10 feet past the hole, well, that is a bigger surprise.

Similar to the EQ Speedometer for properly assessing the emotional temperature and cost, we need an Agnostic Scale to properly asses the cognitive temperature (number of thoughts and their intensity in Hz) so we can make the right adjustments like the Yellow and Red cards did for emotions. The cognitive temperature is like the weight of the luggage, and we know we want to travel light mentally. We know we want the very low frequency alpha waves. Using the simple surprise definition, it is easy to measure what is going on in the brain, just like an EKG machine does.

Agnostic (A) Scale

Please note that in the GYRA Model, the agnostic scale is different from the emotional scale in that the emotional score (GYR) is done per hole, whereas the agnostic (A) score is done per shot. The result of each shot will determine what the brain will be processing. The result of a shot will determine how much luggage will be carried over to the next shot. Next to each shot result is a score from 1 to 10. This is a scale where a small surprise is on the low end of the scale (close to 1) and larger surprises are closer to 10. A "dot" is a perfect shot where the shot and the result were perfect (GSBR).

Here is the Agnostic Scale:

A Score	Result	Typical Response
Dot	Perfect Shot (GSGR)	"Be right!"
1-2	Minor Surprise	"Aahh. It's ok"
3-5	Surprise	"Hmmm. What happened?"
6-10	Major Surprise	"Wow! What was that?"

Here is a description of the Agnostic Scale:

Dot – Perfect: The result was exactly what you intended to do - GSGR.

1-2 – Minor Surprise: Instead of landing in the middle of the fairway, the ball landed about three yards from it, still in the fairway. Instead of the ball landing next to the hole, it landed about three feet farther.

Instead of wanting to chip/pitch the ball on a specific landing spot, you missed it by a couple of inches and the ball is still close to the hole for a tap-in. No big deal, but not perfect. A little Yellow emotionally. No real consequences for the brain to process, but perhaps some wandering over why that happened.

3-5 – Surprise: Instead of landing in the middle of the fairway, the ball landed in the first cut just off the fairway. Instead of the ball landing next to the hole, it landed about 30 feet farther. Instead of chipping/ pitching the ball on a specific landing spot, you missed it by a couple of feet and now you have a tester 3-5-footer left. Definitely Yellow emotionally. Not terrible and a good next shot is all that is required. The brain is wandering for sure and the subconscious is activated.

6-10 – Major Surprise: Instead of landing in the middle of the fairway, the ball is out of bounds. Instead of the ball landing next to the hole, it came up short and is fully buried in the bunker. Instead of wanting to chip/pitch the ball on a specific landing spot, you hit a very poor shot and it is going to be a difficult save from there. Definitely Red. Major consequences are in play here; mind is wandering and subconscious is on fire.

You will note the scale is not equal. 1-2, 3-5, and 6-10 are not equally calibrated. **This is because our longitudinal analysis has revealed a startling causational relationship between these three ranges and impact to the golf (strokes) scorecard**. If no changes are made to the brain, if nothing is done to change the brain frequency or the emotional temperature, then **the golf cost of a surprise for a shot in the 3-5 range is half a shot to the overall score**. This half shot will occur either on the immediate next shot or subsequently on another shot before the round is over. Again, if no changes are made to the brain, if nothing is done to change the brain frequency or the emotional temperature, then **the golf cost of a major surprise for a shot in the 6-10 range is a full shot to the overall score**.

These stroke penalties have nothing to do with the quality of your golf swing, strength of short game, or any other golf skill. In surprise mode, your "negative tendencies" will show up because your subconscious has taken over – you are not in full control of yourself, your conscious brain. **This is why the idea of 'building a golf swing to withstand pressure' is infinitely more difficult than simply knowing how to recognize and dilute the pressure so that whatever swing you have will allow you to perform to your capability.**

In the examples given of the type of surprises per range, let us process them using this new evidence.

1-2 – Minor Surprise: *Instead of landing in the middle of the fairway, the ball landed about three yards from it, still in the fairway. Instead of the ball landing next to the hole, it landed about three feet farther. Instead of wanting to chip/pitch the ball on a specific landing spot, you missed it by a couple of inches and the ball is still close to the hole for a tap-in. No big deal, but not perfect. A little Yellow emotionally. No real consequences for the brain to process, but perhaps some wandering over why that happened.*

Our research did not find any statistical causation or correlation between a slightly mis-hit shot and the score. This is not surprising because the brain is not having to search for any significant explanation for the not perfect shot. So you missed the fairway target by three yards. So what? The brain uses this kind of logic, consciously and subconsciously. There is some luggage, but it is still traveling light for the most part.

3-5 – Surprise: *Instead of landing in the middle of the fairway, the ball landed in the first cut just off the fairway. Instead of the ball landing next to the hole, it landed about 30 feet farther. Instead of wanting to chip/pitch the ball on a specific landing spot, you missed it by a couple of feet and now you have a tester 3-5-footer left. Definitely Yellow emotionally. Not terrible and a good next shot is all that is required. The brain is wandering for sure and the subconscious is activated.*

The brain is warmer, more frequencies are in play taking the brain away from the calm and slower alpha waves. The brain is searching for a reason for this surprise, thus activating the subconscious. Given that all this is happening while on your way to hit the next shot, the signal required for the next shot or a similar shot later in the round will be compromised causing the muscles to not execute perfectly what you want them to.

A tour player called me after a round and said he could not understand why he missed a simple three-foot on the 12th hole. I asked him what were his non-agnostic thoughts and he could not quite come up with any, believing he was indeed agnostic. I asked him to describe that putt. He said it was an uphill inside left cup putt and he left it short. I asked him if he had had any uphill or left cup putts earlier in the round. Upon reflection, he said he missed an eight-foot on the third hole that was also uphill and a little left to right. He had hit that putt too hard and through its break.

Remember, the brain records everything and negative memories are retrieved over positive ones (burnt hand while making coffee). Even though the missed putt on the third hole was probably a 3-5 on the agnostic scale, its impact showed up on the 12th subconsciously. The brain was doing its job. He had not done anything after leaving the third hole, not made any adjustments.

My team and I have had hundreds of these kinds of conversations whilst debriefing GYRA Cards. This is how we know that a surprise of 3-5 for the brain will result in a malfunctioning brain, costing a half stroke. Remember, agnostic (surprise) scores are kept per shot and several of these 3-5 surprise scores could occur on one hole. Each one will have a half-shot cost. I will show you how to keep this kind of a mental scorecard for both the emotional cost and the mental cost as you play. These self-reporting scores will be kept the same way you keep a golf score against par on the same traditional golf scorecard. There is definitely luggage that weighs enough that you can feel it. It is traveling a little heavy now.

6-10 – Major Surprise: *Instead of landing in the middle of the fairway, the ball is out of bounds. Instead of the ball landing next to the hole, it came up short and is fully buried in the bunker. Instead of wanting to chip/pitch the ball on a specific landing spot, you hit a very poor shot and it is going to be a difficult save from there. Definitely Red. Major consequences are in play here; mind is wandering and subconscious is on fire.*

Emotionally you are Red. The brain has way too many active neuropathways with very high frequencies, both required to understand something negative that just happened. The brain is busy retrieving past negative memories or similar mistakes. The brain is far away from the calm and slower alpha waves. The brain is rigorously searching for a reason for this surprise, thus exploding the subconscious. Given that all this is happening while on your way to hit the next shot, the signal required for the next shot or a similar shot later in the round will be compromised, causing the muscles to not execute perfectly what you want them to.

I watched a high-ranking amateur in a tournament who was cruising at three under par when she arrived at a short par-four 14th hole. This hole had a water hazard on the right side of the entire hole. She hit what she thought was a good shot, but slightly blocked it and it ended up in the hazard. She thought the ball may have stopped just short of the hazard as she had used a fairway hybrid to be conservative off the tee in order to keep the good round going. When she got to the spot, she saw her ball in the water. This was a 6-10 surprise. She was startled. She was Red. I could see it. Her subconscious was actively searching for a reason of how a good conservative swing ended up so poor. Her luggage was awfully heavy. She was not traveling light. She took a drop and hit the next shot just short of the green and it rolled back into the water. She made a seven on that hole and went five over par on her last four holes to shoot 77. No rational person can suggest that she mysteriously lost her swing after swinging so well for almost three hours over the 13 previous holes. She had no idea what happened.

The first chapter of this book is full of stories like this. I hear this story over and over again. Everything is fine until something goes wrong, and then, it all falls apart. **Inability to recover is a very common theme**.

Again, remember that the brain records everything and negative memories are retrieved over positive ones. Even though it was a relatively good swing for her off the tee box, and on any other hole without the water would have still been in the fairway, the mental cost of the surprise was very high. She clearly made a poor decision when hitting her subsequent shot, either in her selection of club, or force of strike, target, or properly assessing other risks or variables.

All this work is done in the brain. The same brain that is now processing that surprise that just happened. **The brain was doing its job**. She had not done anything emotional or mental after seeing her ball in the water, thus bringing in a full stroke of penalty into play. In her case, it was much more than a full stroke.

For this, too, my team and I have had hundreds of these kinds of conversations whilst debriefing GYRA Cards. This is how we know that a surprise of 6-10 for the brain will result in a malfunctioning brain costing a full stroke. Remember, agnostic (surprise) scores are kept per shot and several of these 6-10 surprise scores could occur on one hole, as it did for her. Each one will have a full shot cost.

In the next chapter, we will complete the GYRA Mental Scorecard by showing you how to create the cognitive EKG for your brain using the Agnostic (A) language. You already saw how easy it is to convert GYR (emotions, theta waves) into a traditional golf scorecard. I will show you how to keep this kind of a mental scorecard for both the emotional and mental cost as you play. These self-reporting scores will be kept the same way you keep a golf score against par on the same traditional golf scorecard.

Top 3 Ideas

I learned from this chapter

1 _____

2 _____

3 _____

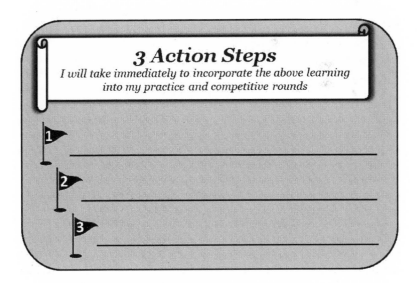

3 Action Steps

I will take immediately to incorporate the above learning into my practice and competitive rounds

1 _____

2 _____

3 _____

Chapter Summary

1. The "A" in the GYRA Scorecard is being Agnostic.

2. Agnostic means "free of" the past and the future. Monologues and narratives are low in frequency enabling alpha brain waves that are required to play in the zone.

3. The brain sends signals to the muscles that are transported via the nervous system. If these signals are too many or of higher frequency (or both), muscle coordination with senses and memory is compromised resulting in poor shots.

4. The brain does not like surprises. In order to make sense of a surprise, the brain goes into search mode. If the surprise is negative, it will search negative memories, mostly in the subconscious.

5. The Agnostic Scale (GYRA Scorecard) is from 1 to 10 indicating a self-reporting surprise number capturing the difference between what you intended to do and what the result actually was.

6. Extensive research shows that a surprise number on a shot of 3-5 will result in a half stroke cost and a surprise number of 6-10 will result in a full stroke cost at some later point in the round, perhaps on the next shot, unless a GYRA Tool (mental strategy) is applied.

7. Agnostic (A) scores are kept per shot (unlike emotional GYR scores kept per hole). Cumulative high surprise numbers can override the brain entirely.

8. Emotions and thoughts (GYRA) are used extensively in golf and are constantly changing with each shot and hole. The ability to change emotions to Green and thoughts to Agnostic is a learnable core skill.

Chapter 5

- *There is quite literally no difference between the current best version of yourself and current worst version of yourself...except the emotional construct of a situation.*
- *If you are learning something to confirm what you already know/ believe ... it's not learning!!*
- *Life is a "maintenance" sport. You have to work on things to grow. You could wake up every morning, hop "on the bike" of life and the view/experience will likely be the same if you are the same person. Every great athlete/person I've known/read about woke up each day & asked, "How am I going to be better than yesterday?"*

@izzyjustice

The GYRA Mental Scorecard

Competition

As is widely espoused by the greats of the game of golf, there are three competitors in the game of golf. In order and sequence, they are:

1. You versus You
2. You versus the course
3. You versus the field

I asked a golfer why we needed to measure any performance? Sounds like a silly question but really worth processing. Why keep score? Why not just hit golf shots until the ball is in each hole until the 18th

hole? Why have par, birdie, bogey, or other scores? If you play in a tournament, why should there be a winner (lowest score against par) or top three, top 10 or even a cut?

We measure human performance so we can gauge where we are, to celebrate if we beat par or a competitor, to know we underperformed if we make bogey or worse, to know what adjustments to make, where to focus practice time, to feel a sense of accomplishment beating others or perhaps our own previous best score. We keep metrics for those competitors.

	Metric
1. You versus You	?
2. You versus the course	Golf Scorecard (against par)
3. You versus the field	Leaderboard

We know the value of metrics in performance, and we have metrics for the second and third tier competition, but not for the primary competitor in golf, yourself. No one is playing defense against you trying to get you to underperform in golf, as in other sports with direct opponents (e.g. tennis). As I wrote in the Introduction and Chapter 1, the primary cause of failure is neither the course nor the field, it is yourself. So why not have a measurement for yourself for the same reasons you have measurements for the other two competitors?

Introducing the GYRA Mental Scorecard

	Metric
1. You versus You	GYRA Scorecard
2. You versus the course	Golf Scorecard (against par)
3. You versus the field	Leaderboard

GYRA is the acronym for Green (G), Yellow (Y), Red (R), and Agnostic (A). Each of one these is noted in a separate row on the same traditional scorecard you would use for any golf course to write down your score against par. Most golf scorecards have multiple rows primarily to keep score for multiple player names in those rows. Score cards typically have columns with yardages per tee box, hole number, handicap of hole, and a cumulative column for score per nine holes, and overall, 18 holes. Since we are going to use this scorecard for individual measurement and not your group's score, you will have to have a separate golf scorecard to keep in your pocket for GYRA score and another, should you wish, for your group score, or simply have someone else do the group score.

You have already seen how the emotional self-diagnosed "EKG" is created over 18 holes. As discussed earlier, your honest self-evaluation is critical to the accuracy of the measurement. Remember, being Green is a rare occurrence. We are rarely in the zone for the entire round, or even a hole. This is why when we are in a zone, we remember it so vividly. If you are feeling normal, that should be considered Yellow.

Going back to Mark and Tyler, if either one of them had written down his GYR score before going to the second hole, a self-measurement, and realized he was Yellow or Red, then that visual inscription of the X on the hole, the "EKG" reading, would have been a sign to change something before the next shot. The "hostage negotiation" with self needs to start. Just like the ideal goal is to shoot better than par on each hole, the goal with GYR should be to try to play in Green, using theta brain waves. **The better goal would be to realize when you are not Green, and make adjustments per hole to get to Green.**

Keep your GYRA scorecards and note how many holes you play in each color. Note what happens after a Red hole if you did nothing versus doing something from what you learned in this book. Golf is a game of mistakes, so the trick will be not so much to avoid mistakes, but to take some action to get back to Green when mistakes do occur.

A few reminders on being Agnostic:

1. You are Agnostic when your brain is free of the past or the future, and focused on the present.
2. Thoughts of the past (what happened) or the future (what could happen) typically generate more brain waves (quantity, mind wandering) and often of higher frequency (intensity, Hz).
3. Thoughts of the past or future occupy the same signal (neuropathway) from the brain to the neuromuscular function as the signal to do what you want to do, thereby compromising the signal leading to a physical error in execution of a shot.
4. The physical error can be anything from hitting something too hard or too soft to having certain muscles out of sequence with others.
5. Not being Agnostic can also result in mental errors over course management as certain variables used to make decisions (lie, wind, pin position, etc.) are missed.
6. The higher the surprise number of the shots, the higher the activation of the subconscious. In competition, during a round, the activated subconscious is likely to seek previous negative experiences to make sense of the perceived threat of the surprise shot.
7. The neurological definition of pressure is the presence of too many thoughts, and mostly negative. The circumstance of a situation creates stimuli for the brain to process primarily subconsciously.
8. It is an incorrect myth to suggest that you can stop thinking, not feel pressure, or not think of the past or future. Our brain is designed to make sense of everything.
9. Therefore, the required skill is to recognize what stimulus creates non-agnostic thoughts, what those non-agnostic thoughts are, and replace them based on the quantity and intensity as you cannot change the circumstance of the situation.

10. Keeping Agnostic Surprise scores per shot will help you know how much needs changing and to use the appropriate tool from this book. You would not use a tool to recover after an "8" surprise as you would after a "2" surprise.

The Agnostic score will have to be captured differently as it is your surprise score after *each shot*. There are several shots per hole, so we have to get creative on capturing the surprise number per hole. Look at just the A row (last row) of the GYRA card below from the same LPGA Tour Player on the same tournament round. Looking at the Agnostic Scores now, you can see why on some holes, where she made birdie (hole 9), she gave herself a Red score. The surprise numbers indicate that it was an emotionally expensive hole, even though she made birdie.

HOLE	1	2	3	4	5	6	7	8	9	OUT	10	11	12	13	14	15	16	17	18	IN	TOTAL
YARDAGE	436	176	451	608	213	410	595	192	452	3533	431	564	239	382	439	180	381	661	460	3737	7270
PAR	4	3	4	5	3	4	5	3	4	35	4	5	3	4	4	3	4	5	4	36	71
ACTUAL SCORE	5	3	4	4	2	3	5	3	3	32	4	4	3	3	3	4	3	5	5	34	
G			x	x	x								x	x	x						
Y		x	x				x				x	x				x	x	x	x		
R	x							x	x												
A																					

Figure 12. GYRA Scorecard: GYR - "A"

Here is the method to capture your A score.

Use the box per hole in the A row to write down clockwise either a dot (GSGR where the result of the shot was exactly what you intended) or a number. Start the sequence of writing down from top left corner of the box and go clockwise for all the shots you have taken, as shown below for just one box.

Let us do a few examples. Take a look at hole 3 on the GYRA card above, which is an actual card we processed. The golfer wrote down the following A scores on a hole where she made par and wrote down Yellow after the hole before going to the fourth hole.

2	5
•	10

For the hole above, a par-four, she told us her drive was not far from her target, thus the 2 score. It was not hit exactly perfect but not bad, in the fairway, just not specifically where intended. The difference in surprise between what she wanted to do and the result was given a 2 by her.

She gave herself a 5 for the second shot. She described her second shot as very poorly struck. She could not understand the cause and could sense her mind wandering increase. The result, however, was not that bad as she did hit the green and was about 20 feet away from the pin for a birdie putt.

For her third shot, her putt for birdie, she said she inexplicably struck it off the toe, something she rarely does, and came up about eight feet. Her immediate, reflexive reaction was to curse at herself. She knew her mind was going crazy, and thus the 10 Agnostic score.

For her par save, she used several GYRA techniques (tools) that will be described later. She putted exactly the stroke she wanted on the line she chose and made the putt dead center. It was a GSGR and a dot. The focus she had on the last putt diluted the impact of the mental cost of the previous hole. She was not Green but not Red, either. Thus, the overall cost of the hole, based on the cost of the shots taken, was Yellow.

We will discuss in Chapter 9 what adjustments she made as a direct result of her GYRA scores and what she did after each shot to make sure she was Green and recovered from non-agnostic shots. In the above example, if she were to go to the next hole and do nothing, she has now brought in the possibility of a full stroke cost (because of the 5 and 10 Agnostic scores) to her overall score either for that day or a proceeding day. There is a very high chance that, should she do nothing, the next time she is facing a similar long putt, or any putt where that came after a poor shot to the green, that her subconscious will retrieve this memory of such a poor putt on the third hole. There is another scenario that could help her, but it is a circumstantial one. If, on the very next hole, she has a similar long putt and drains it, then the memory of the putt on the third hole will be diluted and have less impact down the road. This circumstantial possibility is a risky approach to recover. Remember, positive memories and negative ones are not equal and are not stored in the same place. It takes about five average positive experiences to dilute one negative experience. If she did nothing to recover from the high Agnostic score, she would have to rely on theoretically hitting the next five shots 2 or below on the Agnostic Surprise scale. To leave your performance to circumstance is not the way to performing at your best. It is a gamble in a game (neuroscience) where you are largely ill-equipped to win.

Let us go to hole 11, a par-five.

3	2
•	4

She made birdie on this hole. She told us her tee shot was slightly pulled and that her second shot was actually hit solid but it went farther than she had planned to hit, leaving her an uncomfortable number to pin on her third shot. Sure enough, she blocked her wedge and the ball spun back more than she had thought it would, leaving her a 14-foot right-to-left breaking putt.

She followed her routine, made adjustments based on GYRA tools, studied the break, and struck the ball with exactly the pace she wanted, it broke exactly where she thought it would and went into the cup at exactly the entry-point she had envisioned. She wrote down Yellow after this hole even though she made birdie because only one out of four shots came out the way she wanted. She knew well based on her emotions that she was not in the zone, not in Green. Note again that the golf score at the end of each hole is not always identical to either the emotional cost of the hole or the condition of the brain, its thoughts, and their frequencies.

Let us do one more hole, hole 15, a par-three where she made bogey.

8	6
2	4

This is a hole where she did not make the right adjustments. She said she pulled her iron shot towards a greenside bunker. She could see it was plugged in the sand. A big surprise; she could sense her mind wandering quickly as she had to wait for her other partners to hit before being able to walk to her ball. She said every second of waiting for two other tour players to hit was excruciating because she could sense more thoughts, and negative ones. One of them was, "Don't waste a good round on a simple par-three." She gave herself an 8. Big surprise.

Her plugged lie gave her limited options. She was not focused. She knew it, but felt rushed seeing two balls of her competitors on the green. The ball came out of the bunker, but now had a chip. She thought the ball would be on the green somewhere as hard as she hit it, but it barely came out. A 6 surprise. She was still away and felt even more rushed with her playing partners still waiting on her. She did not make any GYRA adjustments. She hit her chip to about three feet past the hole. She gave her chip a 4 as she missed her landing spot. She made her bogey putt. She gave herself a Yellow on that hole. It was emotionally costly, but she also felt she had a good round going and a bogey would not hurt her. She told us that had she missed her bogey putt, she would have been Red.

The GYRA Scorecard is a mental scorecard that captures your emotional and cognitive state. The status of these two variables plays the largest role in determining whether you can execute a golf shot that you have the skill to.

The first step is to understand what emotions and thoughts are, how they work in the brain, and how to record them as you are playing. The next step is to learn emotional and cognitive techniques, to manage them both so that irrespective of your emotional temperature and surprise number, you can get to Green and be Agnostic. These conditions create those alpha and theta brain waves that allow your brain to command your muscles to do exactly what you want to do, and enjoy every second of being in full control of a moment in time.

You have learned two EQ tools already, the Yellow/Red cards and the ACT breathing technique. In the next few chapters, you will learn more tools so that you can use the GYRA scorecard to recognize where you are and use the right tools for the GYRA score you take.

For the first few times of using the GYRA card, it may feel weird or even time-consuming. Neither will occur if you use the card correctly after that initial phase. We literally took our stop watches out to watch golfers using the GYRA card after each shot and hole. It takes less than 10 seconds to take the card out, write a number, dot or X, and put that card back in your pocket or yardage book. In a four and a half or five-hour round, that is less than 10 minutes total. This is a very nominal time and effort to capture critical data that can be used to make the right adjustments at the right time so that you can perform at your best for the entire 18 holes, not just on holes you *felt* good on. It is data you need to get your mind to be *in the zone*.

The simple act of taking out the scorecard from your pocket and using a pencil to evaluate what happened, itself, is a conscious effort you are making. This alone, whether you do something or not, tells the subconscious that you are in control, that you are not getting attacked by a bear (roar on a hike) and your life is not in danger.

Subsequent actions, which you will learn in the next few chapters, will take it from there and even further reduce the role of the subconscious. This is the competition between you (conscious) and you (subconscious), that you have to consciously win. More importantly, this creates a neurological process that you can duplicate to replicate your success irrespective of the course you play, the competition you have, and the results of the shots you hit.

The GYRA scorecard is also a powerful and more accurate tool to evaluate a round after it is complete. If you are a golf coach and each player who plays in a tournament were to keep this score, it would be so much more data to process than just the raw golf score or the player's narrative. You could identify holes with high Agnostic numbers and realize that from that point on, their brains were not fully functional. Poor swings after high Agnostic scores are to be expected and it would not be because "the swing failed," or "my putter let me down," but because the subconscious took over.

If you are a parent/caddie/player, you can also keep this GYRA scorecard and use it post round to see where a round got away, or what adjustments could be made the next day. It would give parent/caddie/ player a common language to process the round, extract the root causes for poor shots, and make proper adjustments.

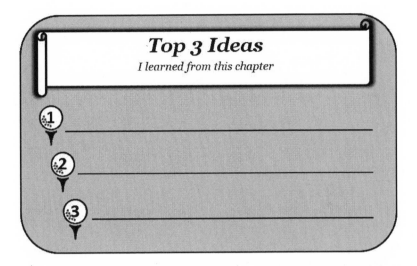

Top 3 Ideas
I learned from this chapter

1. _____

2. _____

3. _____

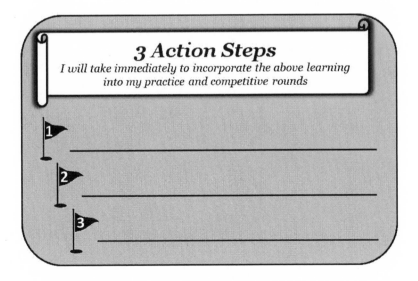

3 Action Steps
I will take immediately to incorporate the above learning into my practice and competitive rounds

1. _____

2. _____

3. _____

Chapter Summary

1. The GYRA Scorecard is golf's first mental scorecard.
2. The GYRA Scorecard is used in real time to analyze where your brain is emotionally and cognitively, creating an EKG-type graph over 18 holes.
3. Golf scores are not necessarily related to GYRA scores. A good score (birdie) can be very emotionally/cognitively expensive. If not addressed, this expense will be even more costly on future holes.
4. A poor score can also not necessarily mean a high cost. Thus, keeping GYRA scores is key to knowing exactly what game time adjustments to make, like good coaches do in timeouts in other sports.

Chapter 6

- *Pain is an interpretation. Sadness is an interpretation. Joy is an interpretation. Everything is an interpretation. You will live a life of a 1000 people if you choose to interpret everything to your advantage.*
- *You are what you think. Your competitor will be grateful if you think you suck.*
- *Who you are as a person gets revealed in competition/sports. It's not the other way around. Being a better person is the price of being a better athlete. Also … the reward.*

@izzyjustice

GYRA Tools – Focus

For this chapter, you will need the following:

1. *A picture, electronic or paper, of anything or anyone*
2. *Something to eat/drink, a small snack-type item*

Now that we have learned about the brain, how it works, how it makes decisions, and the role emotions and thoughts play in your ability to hit a golf shot, let us shift to building tools to make adjustments based on how you score yourself in the GYRA card.

In the next four chapters, I will spend time on pre-tournament, during the round, and post-round strategies, where it matters the most. But before I go there, in this chapter, I will discuss two other key concepts of high performance, not just in golf, but also in life – happiness and focus.

Sports and golf do not create character; they reveal them. Who you are *off* the course will show up *on* the course. It is the same brain, the same software. If you travel heavy off the course, it is going to be really hard to use the tools in the next few chapters to get to Green and become Agnostic. If you are Yellow or Red in life, how can you expect to be Green over a pressure shot in golf?

It is said that exercise has a positive therapeutic effect. This is true physiologically and neurologically. Many athletes and non-athletes tell me that when they are stressed, they go to the gym or for a run or swim and they feel better. This is true, and since there is widespread agreement on this both from a lay-man and scientific perspective, I will not go into the science of it. But golf, even though it lasts five hours, is not a continuously actively athletic form of exercise, like running for five hours, for example. Most of the time, 93% to be exact, a golfer is traveling between shots, waiting on others, or slowly preparing to hit his or her own. All this creates the perfect conditions for the mind to wander should off-the-course life be Yellow or Red. The heavy mental load will return in those non-athletic times during the round.

Happiness

This is quite possibly the least considered variable in all of human performance, not just in athletic or golf performance. Some of you are no doubt skeptical here. You may ask, "What in the world does personal happiness have to do with a three-foot putt?" And it is a fair question. It is infinitely more important, however, that you understand what happiness actually is from a neuroscience perspective.

Some psychologists and philosophers argue that happiness is, in fact, the ultimate pursuit. If you play golf, you do it to make yourself happy. If you work at an office, you do it to make money to do something to make you happy. If you play with your child, you do it to make you happy. If you listen to a song or read a book or watch a movie, at its core, you do it all because *something* inside you makes you feel better. The clothes you chose to wear today, the way you do your hair, what you say – all of it – is an expression of your identity that you hope will either make you directly happy or accepted by others, which itself would make you happy. These are activities that chase the dopamine hormone.

Another way to look at this ultimate pursuit is the converse. Who among you pursues activities that make you unhappy? It could even be argued that we intentionally avoid experiences that we know will make us unhappy. So clearly there is a yin-yang effect here of things that we do or happen to us that either make us happy or unhappy. Some of these things we choose, but many others we do not choose. You can choose to hug your child, but you cannot choose when someone screams at you.

There are countless stories of great athletes who suddenly look like they are clueless while performing, only to later find out that they just lost a loved one a day earlier or a similar personal tragedy. In professional golf, it is not hard to see a decline in performance when a negative life event, such as a divorce or breakup, occurs.

On the other hand, it is also noted that average golfers suddenly perform great when their "personal life is in order". In either case, and so many in between the spectrum of some good or bad experiences of life, the emotional temperature and thoughts off the course play a huge part in being able to be Green and Agnostic on the course. Being happy is not a guarantee of high performance, but it does make it easier to quickly change your temperature and keep those agnostic surprise numbers below 5.

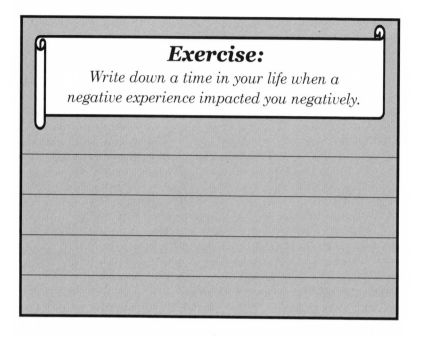

Exercise:

Write down a time in your life when a negative experience impacted you negatively.

Exercise:

Write down a time in your life when a positive experience impacted you positively.

You are encouraged to complete the exercises above before proceeding so that what is next can be personal to you. It is critical for those who seek higher performance to understand the role of happiness in their lives and performance.

The Neuroscience of Happiness

The human body is over 90% fluid. We are essentially a chemical factory with many hormones in our body released from several glands that determine what the composition of "you" is at any given time. The chemical composition of the mix of hormones (emotions) is constantly changing, mostly without your control or knowledge.

Without giving you all a dissertation, let me simplify it down to two dominant families of hormones – dopamine and cortisol. These were labels used in the emotional thermometer. Dopamine is your happy family of hormones (Green) and cortisol is your unhappy family of hormones (Red).

We need cortisol because we need to recognize that a lion is a danger to us, for example, and we must escape quickly from its attack. Until the last 100 years or so, most human beings never traveled more than 50 miles from their place of birth nor lived beyond the age of 40. The sheer volume of stimuli that the brain had to process then versus today is in order of lifetimes. In other words, the people walking the face of the earth today can connect with people and experiences from any other corner of the world. Imagine taking all that stimuli with you wherever you go, with your mobile device constantly feeding the brain with stimuli that, honestly, is mostly negative. This means there is constant cortisol being released in the brain and body. This means it is increasingly difficult to be Green or Agnostic off the golf course. Even though a three-foot putt is just a small white ball going into a hole with hardly any physical strength required, the brain processes that against a vast backdrop of what it is consuming off the golf course and releases the same cortisol-type hormones as though being attacked by a lion.

When the cortisol levels are higher than the dopamine levels, then, generally speaking, we are unhappy. The neurological state of unhappiness is simply that – presence of cortisol over dopamine. Cognitively, this means that our interpretation of any stimulus will inherently be biased (non-agnostic thoughts) using Yellow and Red past memories, not objectively.

New research is showing that four out of five Americans are permanently in this Yellow state because of negative experiences in the past, near past, or currently being experienced. It could have been a traumatic childhood experience, something that happened in a round last week, or a current health issue with you or a loved one, all overlaying on this over-stimulated brain. These experiences release cortisol in your body which creates the stress levels that we call unhappiness. And, as already discussed, the physical body in Yellow or Red state cannot perform optimally to hit a small white ball standing still with a club at 100 mph, where even a slight mis-hit can lead to a flawed shot.

"The biggest rival I had in my career was me." -Jack Nicklaus

Given that golf is a game of misses filled with more disappointments (negative experiences releasing cortisol), the physical body is then constantly compromised to hit a golf ball the way you are capable of. And this does not even take into account all that has happened to you off the course before you started your round.

The idea that happiness can counteract these negative experiences was first explored in performance in the 1920s in the **Hawthorne Experiments**, something worth googling.

These experiments, conducted by Elton Mayo and Fritz Roethlisberger in the 1920s with workers at the Hawthorne plant of the Western Electric Company, were part of an emphasis on socio-psychological aspects of human behavior in organizations. They found that by simply making lights brighter, factory workers *felt happy* and productivity increased. They played music and the same positive impact on performance resulted.

By activating the senses through light and music, visually and auditorily, dopamine levels increased. They could not measure it then, but we can now. We know now that dopamine (Green) facilitates low frequency brain waves of relaxation and cognitively allows the brain to research its positive repository of memories to make good decisions.

It is no secret that we do everything in life better when we are happy. If you are happy, smiling is natural, experiences feel lighter, it is easier to think of new ideas, to remember old ones, to be optimistic, etc. You only need to think of times when you are happy to validate this. It is the same with golf. You just play better when you are happy, and you tend to play not so great when unhappy.

It is part of golf vernacular to hear "Stay in the present" or "Stay in the moment" or "One shot at a time," but rarely has this been decoded with neuroscience, and even rarer, is how to do it beyond just telling someone to do it.

How to be Mindful – Stay in the Moment

"Concentration is a fine antidote to anxiety." -Jack Nicklaus

For the next section, you will need to be very disciplined and follow the instructions very carefully, exactly as prescribed. Otherwise you will compromise your own learning. You will need a picture of anything – a person or a place – and something you can eat like a piece of fruit or power bar of some kind.

Being mindful or being in the present means that dopamine is being released and your neuropathways (thinking) are accessing the right memories and skills for the moment required.

We know that our thinking is a consequence of our emotions (Chapter 2), which, in turn, is a reaction to stimuli. All the changes to that chemical composition of that 90% chemical factory, called the human body, begin with stimuli. Earlier, we learned to trick (self-stimulate) the brain with past positive experiences with the Yellow and Red cards. We learned to reduce the intensity of thoughts by breathing using the ACT Model.

Stimuli enter our cognitive space in only five ways – sight, sound, smell, taste, and feel. All stimuli must go through these channels for the brain to change, for software to be activated. Just as the mouth is the entry for nutritional consumption, the five senses are the entry to what the brain consumes. Is it possible to learn to control what we put in our mouths so that we can control what we nutritionally consume? Of course. The same can be done by training the senses to target what they will allow, to the extent possible, for the brain to process.

To be present, to be in the moment, to be mindful, therefore, is having strong skills with these five sensory channels. It sounds bizarre at first pass to suggest that you are going to learn to see, or hear, or taste, or smell, or feel – we have been doing this since we were born. But how many of you have actually been taught to enhance these skills?

We know people who are blind who have unbelievable hearing skills, but no biological reason for that enhanced hearing skill. They have simply trained themselves to be better at hearing as a necessity. We may also know people who are deaf, but have incredible sense of feel and sight, yet no biological reason for that other than training themselves to be better at them. The point here is that having a better skill over your entry senses is very much possible and you have simply not explored it because you have not had the need to or do not know how to. You will learn now.

This training will help you with your GYRA scorecard. It will be one of the tools you can use to make adjustments based on where you are when you are playing. The good news is that you take your senses with you when you play and they are not considered a training aid by the USGA or R&A!

Sight

I will start with the most powerful of the five senses – sight. Take the picture you were asked to have and look at it. Try to do all these exercises at a time and place where you will not be interrupted.

Exercise:
Five Senses - Sight

Write down three unique attributes of what you see in the picture you chose.

1. _____
2. _____
3. _____

Look at the picture again now, and write down three additional attributes of what you see in that picture.

4. _____
5. _____
6. _____

Look at the picture again now, and write down three additional attributes of what you see in that picture.

7. _____
8. _____
9. _____

Look at the picture again now, and write down three additional attributes of what you see in that picture.

10. _____

11. _____

12. _____

Look at the picture again now, and write down three additional attributes of what you see in that picture.

13. _____

14. _____

15. _____

If you completed each set of the above exercise, you are probably surprised as you thought you could not come up with new unique attributes.

"You can see a lot by just looking." -Yogi Berra

If you went further, you could probably come up with another 15. One of the best ways to practice this is to look at the live face of a loved one – a spouse or child – and come up with 50 unique attributes of his or her face only. It is an advanced skill, but can easily be done with any face. You will find yourself noticing every little feature. And in that moment of looking and searching, your mind is in no other place than the present. **This is how you use sight to be agnostic.**

The effort to keep finding more things to see, a conscious effort, slowly drowns the subconscious, inducing lower frequency waves in the brain and changing your emotional temperature towards Green. This is how you use sight to focus, which I will discuss at length later in this chapter. Just imagine all the things that are available to the eye during a round of golf that you simply do not notice. If you can pick out 15 attributes in just one picture and be agnostic, how many could you pick up on each hole, that could equally keep your mind from wandering and be in the present moment? Imagine how many blades of grass you could see on the line of the putt you want to use? We will discuss more on how to use these senses for the short game in the next chapters.

Feel

The next most powerful sense, meaning this sense has a larger door to the brain and has a significant impact on it, is feel. Just stay wherever you are reading this book and close your eyes before each set and zone in on just feeling something on your body.

Exercise:
Five Senses - Feel

Close your eyes and feel three unique sensations all over your body wherever you presently are. Write them down below.

1. _____
2. _____
3. _____

Close your eyes and feel three additional unique sensations all over your body wherever you presently are. Write them down below.

4. _____
5. _____
6. _____

Close your eyes and feel three additional unique sensations all over your body wherever you presently are. Write them down below.

7. _____

8. _____

9. _____

Close your eyes and feel three additional unique sensations all over your body wherever you presently are. Write them down below.

10. _____

11. _____

12. _____

Close your eyes and feel three additional unique sensations all over your body wherever you presently are. Write them down below.

13. _____

14. _____

15. _____

If you completed each set of the above exercise, you are probably surprised as you thought you could not come up with new unique sensations to feel. If you went further, you could probably come up with another 15.

This is not an advanced skill and can be practiced anywhere, anytime. You will find yourself feeling everything on you, perhaps even the sweat on your head when playing. And in that moment of feeling, touching, and searching, your mind is in no other place than the present. **This is how you use feel to be agnostic**.

The effort to keep finding more things to feel, a conscious effort, slowly drowns the subconscious, inducing lower frequency waves in the brain and changing your emotional temperature towards Green. This is how you use feel to focus, which I will discuss at length later in this chapter. Just imagine all the things that are available to feel during a round of golf that you simply do not notice. Perhaps it is the glove, or your grip or a towel or the dimples on the ball in your hand. If you can pick out 15 attributes in just where you are now, and be present, how many could you pick up on each hole, that could equally keep your mind from wandering and be in the present?

Sound

The third most powerful of the five senses is sound. For this, just stay wherever you are reading this book and close your eyes before each set and zone in on just listening.

Exercise:

Five Senses - Sound

Close your eyes and hear three unique sounds wherever you presently are. Write them down below.

1. _____ Hway _____
2. _____ Creak in wall _____
3. _____ Rub on page _____

Close your eyes again and hear three additional unique sounds wherever you presently are. Write them down below.

4. _____ car _____
5. _____ page turn _____
6. _____ Wind _____

Close your eyes again and hear three additional unique sounds wherever you presently are. Write them down below.

7. _____
8. _____
9. _____

Close your eyes again and hear three additional unique sounds wherever you presently are. Write them down below.

10. _____
11. _____
12. _____

Close your eyes again and hear three additional unique sounds wherever you presently are. Write them down below.

13. _____

14. _____

15. _____

If you completed each set of the above exercise, you are probably surprised as you thought you could not come up with new unique sounds.

If you went further, you could probably come up with more sounds. This is an advanced skill, but can easily be done by practicing literally anywhere, at any time. Eventually, you will find yourself noticing every little sound the way perhaps a skilled blind person does. And in that moment of listening and searching for new sounds, your mind is in no other place than the present. **This is how you use sound to be agnostic**.

The effort to keep finding more things to hear, a conscious effort, slowly drowns the subconscious, inducing lower frequency waves in the brain and changing your emotional temperature towards Green. This is how you use sound to focus, which I will discuss at length later in this chapter. Just imagine all the things that are available to hear during a round of golf that you simply do not choose to hear. If you can pick out 15 sounds just where you are now, and be present, how many could you pick up on each hole, that could equally keep your mind from wandering and be in the present?

Taste

The next sense is taste. For this, you will first need to grab that snack I mentioned earlier, then just stay wherever you are reading this book and close your eyes before each set and zone in on just tasting.

Exercise:
Five Senses - Taste

Close your eyes and take a small bite of whatever you have and eat it the way you normally would, and notice three unique tastes of what you ate. Write them down below.

1. _____
2. _____
3. _____

Close your eyes again, take another bite and this time do it a little slower, allow the food to be in your mouth a little longer, and taste three additional unique tastes. Write them down below.

4. _____
5. _____
6. _____

If you completed each set of the above exercise, you are probably surprised as you thought you could not come up with new unique tastes. If you went further, you could probably come up with more tastes in flavor or texture or the way it sits in your mouth.

This is an advanced skill, but can easily be done by practicing literally anywhere, at any time, and especially when you eat, which for most of us is at least three times a day. Why not practice this every single time you eat? Eventually, you will find yourself noticing every little taste, the way perhaps a skilled person like a sommelier does with wine. And in that moment of tasting and searching for new tastes, your mind is in no other place than the present. **This is how you use taste to be agnostic.**

The effort to keep finding more things to taste, a conscious effort, slowly drowns the subconscious, inducing lower frequency waves in the brain and changing your emotional temperature towards Green. This is how you use taste to focus, which I will discuss at length later in this chapter. Just imagine all the things that are available to taste during a round of golf that you simply do not choose to taste from what you drink and eat. Why waste that experience since you have to do it anyway? If you can pick out six tastes just with one type of food, and be present, how many could you pick up on each hole if you tasted what you drank or ate, that could equally keep your mind from wandering and be in the present?

Smell

This is difficult to do in book format, and in a room or house. It is best to practice this when outside at a restaurant or outdoor event. Do the same thing as the previous four and close your eyes and seek out three new smells at a time until you get to 12.

Exercise:

Five Senses - Smell

Do the same thing as the previous four senses and close your eyes and seek out three new smells at a time until you get to 12

1. _____
2. _____
3. _____

4. _____
5. _____
6. _____

7. _____
8. _____
9. _____

10. _____
11. _____
12. _____

When playing golf, as you approach the clubhouse on the 9th or 18th holes, if you engage your sense of smell, you can pick up many smells. In a PGA/LPGA Tour event, where there are concession stands on just about every hole, it is even easier to engage the sense of smell. And again, by engaging in this sense, you are focusing your mind to respond to the present moment, not wander, giving you a path to lower cortisol by allowing dopamine levels to increase.

"You can win tournaments when you're mechanical, but golf is a game of emotion and adjustment. If you're not aware of what's happening to your mind and your body when you're playing, you'll never be able to be the very best you can be." -Jack Nicklaus

What is critical to understand is that being in the moment, being agnostic over a shot, is a function of your senses. Engaging your sensory organs in this manner allows you to not wander, which, according to Killingsworth's research, is the most powerful way to be "happy" in any given moment.

Emotions and thoughts are the currency with which we seek the ultimate purchase of life, happiness. The game of golf provides an unparalleled opportunity to build skills to use off the course. The skills required to be agnostic over a shot - to feel calm, to feel in total control of the moment with your emotions (Green) and thoughts (alpha/beta waves) to hit exactly the shot you want to hit - is the same skill you need to enjoy life, to be present when having dinner with loved ones, to notice the beauty of life, to feel empowered to change what troubles you, and to feel like your existence is for a purpose.

This is the same physiological mechanism in play when you are on vacation. Oftentimes, you will go to a place like the beach or mountains. If you find that relaxing, the reason is that your senses, all of them, are experiencing a heightened engagement because of the uniqueness of the stimuli of the environment. In other words, the exercises that were just done above with the five senses are happening naturally. Your eyes are looking at the beach, hearing the sounds of the waves, feeling the salty breeze that is common in ocean air. All of these cause you to be in that present moment (agnostic), thinking of what you are experiencing instead of what happened the week before or what needs to happen when you return.

The same is said of artists who go to places to search for inspiration. They might go to a cabin in the mountains, for example. The view of trees, greenery, air, and natural sounds all do the same thing for the artist. They keep him or her present and happy allowing him or her to write the lyrics to the song, or paint, or write a book as alpha and theta waves are naturally induced by what the senses are processing.

What is important to understand is that the inspiration or happiness is happening because senses are engaged fully, and going to a faraway location is a good way of doing it, but by no means the only way. It is possible to be that mindful and inspired wherever you are if you can learn to engage with your senses. The golf course, a place that is often manicured perfectly with large fairways, trees, flowers, ponds, lakes, rivers, and such, is in fact one of the best places to engage with your senses. It is a huge advantage over, say, basketball, where it is always indoors with a sea of fans around or other sporting events that are stadium-style where the stimuli do not change much.

It is impossible, and not necessary, to be a perfectly happy person to perform at a high level, but it is necessary to be able to use your senses to be exactly where you need to be while playing golf so that your negative life experiences do not compromise your ability to execute the shot you are capable of. Being mindful, being present (agnostic), while playing golf by using these techniques is the most effective way to suspend some of life's challenges and concurrently manage your neuropathways and chemical composition to allow you to bring out the best you in you.

In the GYRA Scorecard, you can see now how you can use your senses to change both your emotional temperature and manage any surprise number. Leaving the first green, one new tool for Mark, in addition to the ACT Breathing Model and the cards, could be to look at a flower bed near the second tee box and pick out as many (three more) attributes. Because this is a conscious effort on his part, he is not doing 'nothing' or letting his mind wander to the missed opportunity he just had. He is reducing his subconscious activity.

A flower bed is a low frequency stimulus, thus forcing the brain to reduce the higher frequency negative subconscious thoughts. Tyler could have similarly chosen to take sips from his water bottle, and feel the water in his mouth and feel it even go down his throat. By engaging his feel sense, like Mark did with his sight over the flower, Tyler, too, is doing something conscious. Feeling water in your mouth is a low frequency stimulus for the brain to process.

Because both of them put their emotional score after the hole as Yellow on their GYRA scorecard, they knew they had to do something. Otherwise, their next shot would be compromised. Tyler's surprise numbers were higher than Mark's as he hit more poor shots. Because of this, Tyler needs to do more than Mark to get his brain waves back. He would only know this if he was keeping his agnostic score card in the GYRA card. By having the GYRA card, they know exactly where they stand and what the probability of success is for the next shot, and then make the right adjustments.

"Every great player has learned the two C's: how to concentrate and how to maintain composure." -Byron Nelson

Focus

Let us keeping building our toolkit, learn more ways to be in the zone, to make adjustments when we are not, and to be agnostic.

Being agnostic in the manner described using senses allows you to be focused at the task at hand, and not on the past or future, but in the present moment. Focus is the term often used to describe a golfer who is playing in a zone, executing every shot physically, mentally, and emotionally to the best ability.

Focus, as I see it, is one level below being agnostic. If being agnostic is that exclusive and elusive condition of no thoughts of the past or the future, then being focused is not too far behind that condition. You may have just one or two additional thoughts to be focused. If we can use focus techniques to create the groundwork so that we can be agnostic over the shot, that is ideal. **Think of focus as the garden from which the agnostic fruit can be realized. You do not have to be agnostic when you are walking between shots or waiting for your turn to hit, but you do have to be agnostic over a shot.**

Being in charge of what your brain is consuming is key. The brain is constantly consuming, so why not be in charge (conscious) of what you want the brain to consume?

There are additional ways to reduce mind wandering (subconscious); and having a pre-determined mental diet of what you want your brain to process can be yet another tool.

1. Skill Focal Thought

A skill focal thought is a specific golf mantra related to a technique that you want to focus on. It is one specific golf skill-based form or technique that you can use in your practice or a round to help you glue other skills or to avoid having too many of them. For example, it might be "grip lightly," "release putter," "finish backswing," "smooth transition," or "stay in balance." TURN SHOULDER

Whatever the skill focal thought is, the golf mantra, it is something you can say and think to yourself. It is usually a thought that helps you remember something that you are just learning or often forget to do. These skill focal thoughts need to be simple, no more than three words, and be of such emotional and mental strength that thinking it, or humming it, will reduce mind wandering. A skill focal thought is another conscious way to reduce the subconscious decision-making.

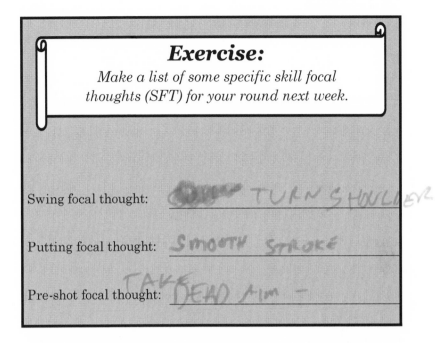

Exercise:

Make a list of some specific skill focal thoughts (SFT) for your round next week.

Swing focal thought: ~~Grip~~ TURN SHOULDER

Putting focal thought: SMOOTH STROKE

Pre-shot focal thought: TAKE DEAD AIM —

"All that we are is the result of what we have thought" –Buddha

2. EQ Focal Thought

Similar to the skill focal thought, an EQ focal thought is much simpler. It is an *emotional* focal thought. It usually is just one word or a very short phrase mantra for that specific round. Some examples my clients have used are names of their kids, parents, favorite place, hometown, favorite food, or even a cliché like "travel light," "don't give up," "stay Green," or "be thankful." Its purpose is to get you to relax (Green) and even enjoy your round. It may also be the name of your collegiate mascot, your favorite pro golfer, your favorite course, your goal, your favorite color, or anything that works for you.

The purpose of your EQ focal thought is to have an operating emotional mantra to hum to or think of or feel for the entire round no matter what happens that you know will have an impact in changing your emotional temperature and allow you to be agnostic over a shot. These mantras can be used between shots consciously as fertilizer for being Green when you get to your next shot. Change it up for each round or practice session.

Exercise:

Make a list of all the EQ focal thoughts that come to mind and use them for your next round.

1. 2 DORNOCH
2. 1 JANNIE
3. GIRLS
4. OLLIE
5.
6.
7.
8.
9.
10.

"Confidence in golf means being able to concentrate on the problem at hand with no outside interference." -Tom Watson

3. Macro Focus

As part of a new language to make adjustments with your GYRA scorecard as you battle the competition of you versus you, the term "macro focus" describes another tool to use. You have 14 golf clubs in your bag, each to hit a different kind of shot. Why not have several EQ and mental tools that you can also use in different situations based on where you are on the GYRA card?

Macro focus is an emotionally light way to stay Green using your senses as described earlier. It may be to notice the trees, clouds, wind, lawns, ponds, flowers, and such. Macro focus is the type of focus *required* as soon as you enter the golf course property. Once you pass the gate of the entrance to the golf course, you are now a golfer. You are no longer all your other roles in life. It is time to enter your performance arena, and starting with macro focus is recommended.

A fundamental premise in focus is that a *conscious* effort to think about one thing is a *subconscious* effort to not think about another thing.

If you choose to notice the big oak tree by the gate of the entrance of the golf course, you are subconsciously choosing to not think about what happened off the course earlier or have to do afterwards. You can use all your senses to macro focus. It is important to keep this focus (macro) light and make sure it is not the type that drains you emotionally or mentally. It can be smelling the hamburgers being grilled, the shape of clouds, the feel of wind on your body, or hearing birds chirp. This is all light and allows you to be present as described earlier.

During the round, macro focus should be one of the tools to use **between all shots**. This should complement your EQ focal thought. In the next chapters, we will learn additional tools to use between shots. They will be different from tee box to fairway, from fairway to green, and on and around the greens. Having these tools will allow you to choose which ones fit the right EQ temperature of the hole, and how to adjust the surprise numbers.

"Everything was fine, until I walked onto the first tee!" -Seve Ballesteros

4. Micro Focus

Micro focus is different from macro focus in that micro is a much deeper focus, not light at all. It is a laser-type of focus on a very specific task or spot. It is a deeper engagement of the senses to fully be agnostic. The purpose of macro focus is not to be agnostic, as much as it is to prepare to be agnostic. Micro focus, on the other hand, is definitely used to be agnostic and, therefore, better for your pre-shot routine or when over the ball.

An example is to use sight skills to notice not the ball you are about to strike, but a very specific dimple where you want the club face to hit. It might also be to feel the grip in every part of your hand and fingers, or to feel your feet in your shoes sensing every inch of the ground underneath. It can even be to sense the saliva in your mouth or quality of air going into your mouth and lungs. When you are over the ball, about to strike, that is the time when all the focus has to be on the shot needed to be executed and nothing else.

This is the proverbial *moment of truth*, where a non-agnostic thought can come out from nowhere. If you are over the ball, have done everything to be agnostic, and suddenly your subconscious says, "Don't go left," other than backing off the shot and restarting, there are limited conscious actions to take to negotiate with the subconscious and subdue it so you can have those clear electric waves going from your brain to your muscles.

Non-agnostic thoughts will interfere with that signal and cause a muscle or two to be out of sequence or have the incorrect sense of force or speed since the brain is now processing this "threat" of not going left. Thus, micro focus using the senses to replace the "Don't go left" internal interruption is possibly the only tool to use, perhaps along with the ACT breathing tool.

What if you are over the ball and about to hit your shot and your caddie says to you, "Don't go left"? You would clearly understand that it is a disruption to your brain, and your ability to hit your shot the way you want to has been compromised. Everyone who heard your caddie say that to you would completely understand how irresponsible and distracting it was for the caddie to do that. **Yet, golfers do this to themselves all the time.** Some version of "Don't go left" mysteriously comes up. Only now we know the brain does nothing randomly and the subconscious retrieved that thought from somewhere in your brain.

It is imperative that you not attempt micro focus until you are either in your pre-shot routine or over the ball about to hit it. Using micro focus between shots will consume neuropathways that you really want to save for when you are over the ball. Between shots is when to use macro focus, the light brain waves using all senses just to ready your emotions and thoughts for micro focus.

As noted earlier, every bad shot you hit, which is defined as not executing on a shot you know how to hit, can be first traced to your emotional temperature and your ability to be agnostic over the shot. No change to your golf swing or equipment should be made unless the pattern of your bad shots is consistent.

I have had very healthy debates with golf instructors on this matter. There is a paradigm of creating a golf swing that can withstand pressure situations. At this point in the book, you should know that pressure exists in the brain, not the muscles. Using the EQ and mental tools changes the pressure so you can use whatever swing got you there in the first place. If you are in a pressure situation, a chance to win a tournament on the back nine, clearly you did many things right to get there. Clearly the only thing different about the back nine on Sunday to win a tournament on tour and the back nine on Thursday, other than weather conditions and pin placements, is the activity going on in your brain. Performing poorly in pressure situations and then changing your swing or equipment is like using a hammer on a screw. These changes are not fixing the problem.

In every example given in Chapter 1, of all the surprise stories in golf and other sports, it should be clear that the subconscious emotions and thoughts were the real problems. If you miss a three-foot putt to lose a tournament, what good is it to practice three-footers, or to change the putter, or to use a different grip? You could make all these changes during practice and make all the three-footers, but those practice three-footers used a brain that could not be more different than the one you had when you missed.

The ability to have a measurement system to know exactly where your emotions and thoughts are when you hit a shot and play a hole, an "EKG" of your brain, is critical to fixing the right problem. Medical doctors and nurses ask several questions and conduct many tests on you to make sure they have a proper diagnosis first. There are many drugs and remedies, but they have to pick the right ones for your specific medical condition. Properly identifying the problem for their patients using all kinds of data is standard operating procedure. Golfers use their brain on every shot, between shots, in practice and off the golf course. It should always be the first place to look to see if the problem originated there.

If you keep the GYRA scorecard and notice that you played the round in Yellow and/or Red, the proper diagnosis should be that you were:

1. Unable to focus
2. Unable to be calm, relaxed, and enjoy the round
3. Unable to make the right adjustments

If you read your own self-reported Agnostic numbers and notice many 5 or above numbers, the proper diagnosis should be that you were:

1. Mind wandering a lot (too many thoughts)
2. Your subconscious was very active
3. Unable to be agnostic, or hold one focal thought
4. Unable to make the right adjustments

The GYRA scorecard will reveal all this to you per hole and per shot. You can go back to it after a round and validate the measurements you took. You will know how you did against yourself. Win this, and you give yourself the best chance to win the competition against the course and the field. My phone rarely rings when a golfer loses against the field or the course. It rings when the golfer feels he or she is beating him/herself, underperforming, unable to bring to competition what he or she can easily do on the range and in practice.

The GYRA scorecard begins to answer a key question asked by a Tour Professional: "What do I need to do to get mentally stronger?"

Consider a study by Dr. Gail Matthews on accomplishing goals. Take a look at the table below.

	Group 1	Group 2-3	Group 4	Group 5
Think about goals	✓	✓	✓	✓
Write about goals	✗	✓	✓	✓
Share with a friend	✗	✗	✓	✓
Weekly progress report to friend	✗	✗	✗	✓
Success Rate	43%	56%	64%	76%

Table 1. Achieving Goal Success

This is a general study on simply having goals. It shows that if you write your goals and have a progress reporting mechanism, something to analyze and share, there is a 76% higher probability to achieve that goal. Knowing you have to be Green and Agnostic is the goal. Sharing your GYRA card with yourself and someone else allows you to know what to do to become mentally stronger. I know my clients are getting mentally strong when I see their Agnostic numbers become lower, when they rarely get in Red, and if they do get in Red or have a high surprise number, the subsequent shot or hole is back towards Green and lower numbers. Using GYRA tools, which we will discuss in the next chapter, and using them correctly at the right time based on your GYRA scores, is what you have to work on to become mentally stronger.

"Success does not consist in never making mistakes, but in never making the same mistake twice" -George Bernard Shaw

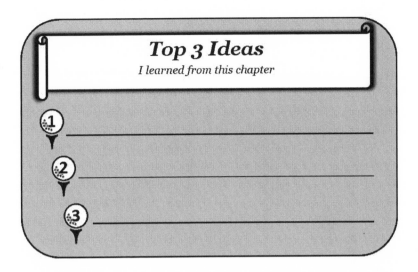

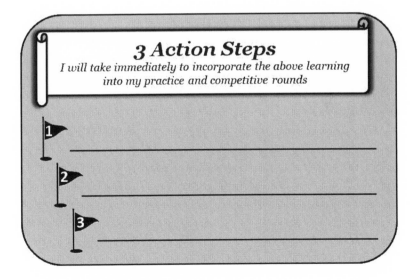

"Tell me and I forget, teach me and I may remember, involve me and I learn." -Benjamin Franklin

Chapter Summary

1. Happiness is a chemical body state associated with high performance.
2. Being Agnostic is a neurologically proven technique to be happy in the moment, increasing dopamine over cortisol and allowing your body to mentally recall a skill and physically execute a shot.
3. The five senses are under-utilized assets that can be used to be Agnostic.
4. The golf course is a great place to engage all your senses to be Agnostic.
5. Skill focus thoughts, EQ focal thoughts, Agnostic focal thoughts, macro and micro focus are all GYRA tools that can be used to change GYR and A readings on the GYRA Scorecard.
6. A conscious effort to do one thing is a subconscious effort to *not* do something else. GYRA tools are all a conscious effort on your part that concurrently dilutes the role of the subconscious.

Chapter 7

- *Doing things others do is copying. Not doing things because no one has done it is cowardly. Neither helps you reach your potential.*
- *The first step to improvement is accepting that what you know is not enough.*
- *The brain is never doing nothing.*

@izzyjustice

GYRA Tools – Tournament Week

In Chapter 8, I will share specific examples of using the GYRA scorecard and making specific adjustments during your round per GYRA score per shot and per hole. In Chapter 10, a Tour Professional will share how he used all these tools from his GYRA golf bag, a toolbox of EQ and mental tools, to get through the second stage of Qualifying School. These very application-oriented and situation-specific chapters will allow you to go out there, build your own GYRA bag, and pick out the right tool to use for the right situation to allow you to be Green emotionally and Agnostic mentally.

"Winning is not always the barometer of getting better." -Tiger Woods

At this point, you have learned that:

1. 93% of your time playing golf is spent not hitting a shot.
2. Golfers say 60-95% of golf is mental.

3. Pressure is a neurological state of too many thoughts and high frequency thoughts (negative).

4. Being in a zone is having few thoughts and low frequency thoughts of alpha and theta brain waves.

5. Given standard mind wandering is 65% and our subconscious makes 80-95% of decisions, the real competitor in golf is a battle between you (conscious) and you (subconscious).

6. Learning to asses where your emotions and thoughts are at any given point allows you to then use tools from the GYRA bag to make adjustments to get to Green, be Agnostic, and perform to your capability.

In this chapter, we will focus on adding more tools to the GYRA bag. The tools already in the GYRA bag are:

1. ACT Breathing
2. Yellow and Red Cards
3. EQ Speedometer for taking your Emotional Temperature
4. GYRA Scorecard: An Emotional and Mental Accounting system
5. Focal Thoughts: EQ, Golf and Mental
6. Macro and Micro focus

In my last book, *Golf EQ*, I discussed ways to practice, what to do in the days leading to your competitive round, warm up, and post round. I will not repeat that information, but it might be worth perusing to get ideas. In this chapter, we will focus on very specific tools in a sequence.

The central premise of all these tools is to realize that 75% of what it takes to be Agnostic over a shot must be done before getting over the ball.

In order to be agnostic over a ball, to be in no other place mentally other than that very specific moment in time, and have no non-agnostic thoughts while feeling Green, calm and focused, the majority of the work has to be done before the shot. The brain is constantly consuming stimuli, interpreting them in a very biased manner using only your own memories of experience and knowledge. It is very important to have as much control over what you want coming into your brain through those five doors, your five senses.

This process needs to begin in earnest 24-48 hours before your round. This time used correctly should be converted into Green "fertilizer" for the brain so that 24-48 hours later, it will be easier to use other tools. If you are dealing with chaos and engaging in high frequency thoughts, negative experiences, in the days leading up to the tournament, it will be infinitely harder for the EQ tools to work. I realize life is life and we cannot simply change the fact that, for example, our Dad is in the hospital or a child is sick or a marriage is in crumbles or that your last tournament was a disaster. Whether these circumstances are there or not, going into a full brain-cleansing mode is a key tool. I call it having an EQ Diet.

EQ Diet

Wrestlers and boxers often need to be in a certain weight class before their match. Depending on what they weigh several days before, they then get on an aggressive nutritional diet to meet the desired weight. As a golfer, you want to be as Green as possible before tournament day and have as many low frequency brain waves as possible. This is a mental target for you to achieve, just as a fighter does for his physical weight. Managing all that your brain is consuming in that 24-48 (or more) hours before your key round is going to have to be a skill you will need to learn and have the discipline to constantly execute.

In tournaments where there are multiple rounds, this EQ Diet will need to extend to post-round activities and next day activities.

During the 24-48 hours pre-tournament phase, the focus on golf skills needs to diminish each day and, concurrently, the focus on the EQ Diet should increase leading up to game day.

There are two key parts to a good EQ Diet:

1. Increase Green Activities
2. Eliminate Red Activities

It really is that simple. Green activities are experiences you know will move your EQ Speedometer needle towards Green. They are experiences where the thoughts in your brain to process the stimuli of the Green activities are low intensity (Hz) ones. Red activities are those that will move the needle in the EQ speedometer towards Red. Remember, it takes five Green experiences to dilute one Red one on average. Red activities increase your cortisol levels. This is happening naturally in your body. The more this chemical is in your body, the harder it is to dilute. Once the tournament starts, to expect that you can suddenly start from scratch, like turning on your laptop, is to leave your success to chance. You may perform well, but there is a higher likelihood that you will either have an average performance or underperformance.

In the days leading up to your tournament round, substitute the physical training time with EQ training time. **This EQ Diet is also called filling up the EQ Tank**. Here are some examples of what you can do:

1. Practice taking your EQ temperature every hour by imagining there is a permanent invisible EQ speedometer over your head.
2. Make current your Yellow and Red cards.
3. Practice using your cards.
4. Engage in conversation with people who you know will be encouraging and have positive dialogues.

5. View every experience as one that can make you Green or Yellow. By taking your temperature, having the EQ speedometer over your head, proactively steer yourself toward Green experiences and steer away from Yellow experiences.

6. Fine tune your suggested monologues for the round, and practice them on your EQ Diet days.

7. Begin Macro Focus through the week so that on game day, you are already used to it.

8. The night before the round, if you are not sleeping, then instead of letting your thoughts wander, engage in very strong visualization exercises where you recall past good rounds or past positive experiences of your life (in sport or life in general).

9. Practice light meditative yoga, using very low intensity poses in conjunction with light soothing music, and practice A and C breathing in the ACT Breathing Model.

10. The golden EQ rule is to engage in positive activities, the kinds that make you feel very good about yourself, cause you to smile, laugh, and be joyful.

Exercise:

Make a list of 10 activities you can do during pre-tournament days that can fill your EQ Tank.

These can be anything from watching your favorite movies, reading inspiring books, eating foods you love, talking to people who will be supportive, etc.

1. _____

2. _____

3. _____

4. _____

5. _____

6. _____

7. _____

8. _____

9. _____

10. _____

Exercise:

*Make a list of 5 activities to avoid
during pre-tournament days.*

*You know from past experiences that these will deplete your EQ
Tank. These can be anything from negative people in your life,
to activities that are stressful or events that require significant
amount of your EQ.*

1. _____

2. _____

3. _____

4. _____

5. _____

Agnostic Diet

Remember, the real test of your round does not really start until
something goes wrong, when a surprise occurs. That is when the real
tournament and battle begins between you and you.

*"It's never easy to win but it's a lot easier to win when you play well. The
key is winning tournaments when you are not playing so well." -Rory
McIlroy*

The brain does not like surprises. They are fuel for mind wandering and ignite the subconscious. All great athletes have a plan for what will go wrong. They do not want the first time their brains are having to deal with a surprise to be during the round. If somehow the brain can rehearse surprises before the round, then if or when they occur, even though it is still a surprise, the agnostic number will be low as the brain has rehearsed it. This is building the Agnostic Diet.

Below is a list of some common surprises that can happen before a round. Regrettably, one or more of these will likely happen to you. **It is better to have thought through how you will address the mishap beforehand so your brain has a solution to go to instead of wandering through its negative memory bank when you are playing.** As you review this list, make a note of how you will address them if they were to occur to you. You may already know how to address some of them, but may not know how to address others. The only way to know for sure that you are prepared is to address them in practice rounds. If you do not have the knowledge or skill to address the issue, then work with your coach, peers, golf professionals, or seek information from the internet (YouTube is an excellent source of "how to" information) and try it in practice. Your candor in this exercise will only serve you well.

"I've missed more than 9,000 shots in my career. I've lost almost 300 games. 26 times, I've been trusted to take the game winning shot and missed. I've failed over and over and over again in my life. And that is why I succeed." -Michael Jordan

Potential Pre-Tournament Surprises

1. Fatigue due to over training (too much time on golf), anxiety, or lack of sleep.
2. Upset stomach or another ailment.
3. Inability to eat normal food.
4. Something is missing in your golf bag.

5. Traffic delays result in little time to do normal warm up.
6. Seeing that you are paired with someone you do not like.
7. Other players wanting to over socialize.
8. A loved one is in dire circumstance.
9. Feeling stiff, forgot to stretch or warm up before round.
10. Did not prepare for changes in weather (rain, colder or warmer than forecasted, etc.).

"Success is going from failure to failure, without loss of enthusiasm." – *Winston Churchill.*

Exercise:

Make a list of 10 pre-tournament surprises that could happen to you in the days leading to a tournament.

For each one, think of a solution. Then, during practice, purposefully induce one or more of these surprises and see if your solution would work.

1. Surprise:
   Solution:

2. Surprise:
   Solution:

3. Surprise:
   Solution:

4. Surprise:
   Solution:

5.	Surprise:
	Solution:
6.	Surprise:
	Solution:
7.	Surprise:
	Solution:
8.	Surprise:
	Solution:
9.	Surprise:
	Solution:
10.	Surprise:
	Solution:

"You're going to make mistakes. The key is to learn from them as fast as possible and make changes as soon as you can. That's not always easy to do because ego and pride get in the way." -Tiger Woods

Agnostic Diet – Decision-Making Preparation

Your brain is going to be making tons of decisions as noted in Chapter 2. You are going to have to process hundreds of data points to make many decisions. Decision-making preparation is similar to preparing for the surprises above, in that, if you can either make or have processed, in advance, decisions you will have to make on the course come game day, then this will also reduce surprise numbers. It is easier to make an adjustment from a plan that your brain has versus your brain trying to make a plan as you go along. Doing the latter will increase your brain waves (number of thoughts) and if there are any decisions that have to be made on the course using unknown data, like hitting a blind shot, then the intensity of the brain waves will also be high. This will take you far away from being agnostic.

It is key to have a course management strategy of how you will play each hole and then deviate from that "Plan A" if conditions or circumstances change. I realize that having a course management strategy is not new advice, any PGA teaching professional will tell you that, but hopefully you now have a different reason for believing in this sage advice.

For each hole, you must have an idea of what club you plan to hit, and where you want the ball to end, so that you can best attack the green or pin position. This will differ for each hole, each golf course, and even each day when conditions often change. Write down this strategy in your yardage book along with a Plan B. There are numerous resources already available to help you do this. As such, this book will defer to those subject matter experts.

Exercise:

Make a list of 10 decisions you can make in advance of your tournament to minimize the surprise to prepare for your tournament.

1. _____
2. _____
3. _____
4. _____
5. _____
6. _____
7. _____
8. _____
9. _____
10. _____

Sleep

There has been a ton of new neuroscience regarding the relationship between sleep and both physical and mental performance. There are some wonderful books and YouTube videos on this subject that

I encourage you to explore. Circadian rhythm is a good search term to use.

The bottom line is that sleep time is a critical time for the brain to "resurface" its neuropathways. We use these "roads" to process what is happening on the course and make decisions. There is a current that travels on them when we are awake to process all the constant stimuli. Sleep is the time when stimuli are reduced and proteins can go "resurface" them so that good thinking and decision-making can occur.

With everything you now know about the brain, you know why you must have a fresh brain for your tournament. Sleeping in on those one or two days before a tournament is arguably the most important activity to take seriously and not compromise under any circumstance.

Some good habits include:

1. Turning off all electronic stimuli at least two hours before sleep. Shower and get in bed at least one hour before anticipated sleep.
2. Dark rooms with cooler temperatures are preferred.
3. Listening to light music or reading a relaxing book can be done in the last hour.
4. Reading how you might manage surprises in advance is very good. This puts the brain in an *empowered* state.
5. Closing your eyes and visualizing your Yellow and Red cards should be done.

"Golf is evolving, every day, every shot." -Tiger Woods

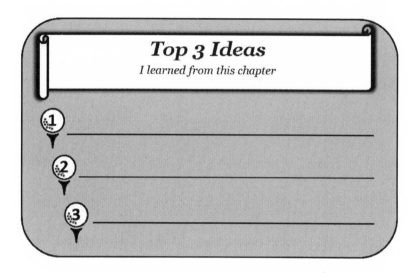

Top 3 Ideas
I learned from this chapter

1 _____

2 _____

3 _____

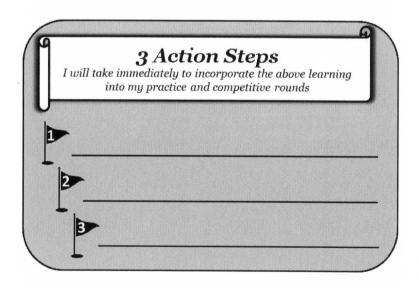

3 Action Steps
I will take immediately to incorporate the above learning into my practice and competitive rounds

1 _____

2 _____

3 _____

Chapter Summary

1. The central premise of all these tools is to realize that 75% of what it takes to be Agnostic over a shot must be done before getting over the ball.

2. This begins with having a strict plan and an emotional and cognitive diet one to two days before a key tournament round.

3. An EQ Diet, managing what emotions you want your brain to consume, is a function of actively increasing Green activities and equally important, eliminating Red activities. This is called filling up the EQ Tank that will invariably be depleted as competition starts.

4. An Agnostic Diet, managing what thoughts you want your brain to consume, is primarily about rehearsing mentally all the surprises (which the brain does not like) and solutions, so that on the course is not the first time your brain has to process the surprises.

5. It is better to have thought through how you will address the surprise beforehand so your brain has a solution to reference instead of wandering through its negative memory bank when you are playing, which will compromise being Agnostic on the course.

6. Sleep is a *requirement*, not an activity, for your brain to be rested in order to make good decisions on the course. It should be viewed as critical as having 14 golf clubs in your bag. Having a sleep routine one to two hours before actual sleep time must be developed and strictly adhered to.

Chapter 8

- *You can improve any situation by simply offering the most empowering narrative of the situation.*
- *If it's easy, everyone will do it. Don't do what everyone does.*
- *A sense of constant awareness and observation using your senses is truly one of the best gifts you can give yourself. It's the easiest way to expand your travel mentally while standing in the same spot.*

@izzyjustice

GYRA Golf Bag – Tools for Competitive Round

In this chapter, we will keep building our GYRA golf bag, creating more tools for use to change our EQ Speedometer to Green and to travel light mentally. In the last chapter, we discussed how important it is that, in order for these tools in the GYRA bag to work optimally, a brain cleanse should be considered a non-negotiable requirement. Good sleep prepares the thinking roads we need. An EQ Diet dilutes cortisol levels before the round, creating an emotional advantage over your subconscious. An Agnostic Diet of rehearsing surprises and course management creates lower surprise numbers, less mind wandering, diluting the neurological condition commonly known as pressure. This preparation gives you the best chance to start the round traveling with a light load, and to keep it light over five-plus hours on the endurance test part of golf.

Game Day Tool 1: 5-S

This is simple. We did this in our warm up and in Chapter 6. It is simply stopping for a moment and reactivating the five senses in this sequence: *Taste, Smell, Sound, Feel, Sight.* The idea is to find only one attribute from the present moment in the specific place you are for each sense. It should take no more than a few seconds and will redirect neuropathways away from the subconscious and reduce the intensity of higher frequency (negative) brain waves.

This is a tool that can be used anywhere, anytime, on the course during the round, but especially recommended for short game shots.

Game Day Tool 2: Slow Breath, Walk and Thoughts

Once a tournament starts, everything feels faster. I have had countless conversations where golfers of all levels have told me that "things speed up," and even though there is a walk involved between shots and it is five-plus hours, it just *feels* fast. It is important to understand this phenomenon from a neurological perspective.

One second is always one second. It is simply that whether you are at the beach taking a nap or playing golf. Yet, golfers - and athletes in general - are right in observing that *it just feels faster*. Alpha and theta brain waves, the ones associated with being in the zone/agnostic, are very low frequency waves. In these waves, time actually feels slower. As a matter of fact, "everything feels very slow" is one of the more common attributes of being in the zone.

The more brain waves and/or the more intense (higher frequency, Hz) brain waves, the faster time feels. This is because, once a round begins, the sheer volume of new stimuli is dramatically more. There are just more stimuli present for your brain to process. The increased stimuli in conjunction with a game-time clock is suddenly too much for the brain to process, creating the feeling of time being fast. What is fast is actually too many stimuli to process, to many decisions to make, and being on the clock at the same time.

When you are on the range, there is no time clock. You do not have to wait for another person to hit. You do not have to mark your ball. You do not have to be aware (awake senses) about being on someone's line. You do not have to be aware about the consequence of your shot. You do not have to keep another golfer's score. You do not have to worry about fans in the gallery.

I can go on and on to belabor the point that once a round starts, however, make no mistake, because of all the new stimuli, your brain goes from 0-60 mph instantly (like a car) and stays there. **A key symptom of being under pressure (too many thoughts and mostly negative ones) is almost always a loss of calibrated speed**. Swings become faster in transitions and putts are hit too soft or too hard. There are too many thoughts in competition with your conscious one (what you intend to do with a shot) that the electric signal from the brain to the muscles is compromised.

A key tool in the GYRA bag has to be to **slow down**. You can do this by:

1. Taking more abdominal breaths in the ACT breathing model. This consciously controlled neuromuscular action will send signals to the brain that you are not in real danger (real as in a lion is about to eat you).
2. Walk slow. I understand that you have to keep walking in golf to your next shot, but given the opportunity, perhaps as you wait for your partner to hit or around the greens, just take steps at a slower pace. Even taking a slightly slower pace than what you are subconsciously doing will have a similar effect neurologically as taking abdominal breaths.
3. Think slow. I often have my golfer hum a song or tune very slowly as though the battery on his or her radio is dying and

the music is coming out real slow. Because this is again a conscious action, it reduces the subconscious activity (number of thoughts) and even intensity of those negative monologues.

Mark and Tyler could both have done any of the above as an adjustment strategy after their first hole. Tyler could have done this after each of his poor shots. It is not a guarantee that his subsequent shots would have been better, but it sure decreases the probability of a poor subsequent shot.

These are tools for you (conscious) to beat you (subconscious).

Game Day Tool 3: 10-2 Tension

Another symptom of pressure, along with everything feeling fast is the loss in calibration of force. With too much stimuli to process, the brain has too much competition to be accurate with its sense of speed (how fast/slow to hit the ball) and force (how hard/easy to hit the ball).

Grab any club if it is near you and if not, take your hands and put them over each thigh. Now squeeze as hard as you can for about five seconds and "record" what that tension felt like all over your body. Give that recording a 10. Based on this maximum tension, grab your club or your thighs again and this time squeeze until it feels like a 2.

Be aware that for all clubs and all shots, the tension you want to feel all over your body, not just your grip, is about a 2. We have observed clearly that alpha and theta waves operate best when the tension in the neuromuscular functions are around 2, which is congruent with the low frequency of those two brain waves.

When playing, I recommend to do this with your club at least once a hole, and for sure, at any time you record a 5 or more on the Agnostic scale or are in Red. I especially recommend it before having to make a crucial putt, as speed - and not line - is usually the culprit. This simple 10-2 Tension will "recalibrate" the brain's sense of force, and though not a guarantee of a great next shot, it does for sure reduce the probability of hitting a poor shot.

Sam Snead famously said to grip it like you are holding a bird. He was right even though he may not have known the neuroscience behind it. What we are doing with the 10-2 Tension tool is to be able to do it repeatedly over the course of the round.

Game Day Tool 4: The 3-Ps

Speed and force recalibration happen only in the brain. It is the brain that decides how hard or soft to hit a ball, not a muscle. It is the brain that decides how fast or slow to swing, not the muscle. You now know how to recalibrate both. Golf is a game of inches, they say, and any ball hit even slightly with the unintended speed or force will result in a poor shot, and perhaps a stroke on that shot.

Unfortunately, there will be competition in your brain to effectively do either recalibration, speed and force. The cumulative effect of shots from when the round began, the emotional and agnostic cost of shots, can dilute your ability to recalibrate later in the round in the tournament week.

The 3-Ps is an acronym for 3 positives. It is a "clean as you go" tool for each shot to reduce the cumulative impact/cost of the previous shots on your present one.

After each shot, your subconscious has instantaneously already judged the shot and created a commentary. Whether the shot is good or bad, your subconscious has spoken.

Here are some narratives that instantly do make it out of the brain:

1. What a shot!
2. Be right!
3. Kick left!

4. Kick right!
5. I suck!
6. Damn it!
7. Common wind!
8. Let it go wind!
9. I could not have hit that any better!
10. No way that putt goes left?

Take a moment to neurologically analyze any one of these subconscious verbalized reactions. If this is what came out, how much more is still kept inside? If this is what came out, what memories were used to make that comment, good ones or bad ones? If this is what came out, what is the level of luggage in the brain? What is the intensity (Hz) of these comments? What is the EQ speedometer reading?

There are also dozens of non-verbal reactions that the subconscious orchestrates, e.g. a fist pump, throwing of clubs, slamming of clubs, looking down, looking up, raising hands in despair, and so on. The same questions can be asked.

"There is no room in your mind for negative thoughts. The busier you keep yourself with the particulars of shot assessment and execution, the less chance your mind has to dwell on the emotional." –Jack Nicklaus

It should be noted that all these reactions are from the subconscious, the competitor of the conscious. The 3-Ps allow the conscious to dictate the narrative. **You should assume that every single shot you hit already has been processed by the subconscious**. So, what is the conscious going to do?

The 3-Ps are three very short positive facts specific to the result of the shot you just hit. They are not generic positives about you, your loved ones, the world at large (acknowledging there are positives in all of them, too). No. The 3-Ps have to be regarding this moment in time.

Let us take two shots from Mark and Tyler. Mark's first two shots on the par-five were spectacular. His subconscious naturally said something positive. When he missed his first putt, his subconscious was ignited. It started doing exactly what it is designed to do: it started its negative narrative. Mark could have used the 3-Ps like this:

1. I can still make birdie.
2. I just hit two amazing shots a few minutes ago.
3. I saw what the ball did going past the hole.

This conscious narrative subdues the subconscious narrative, reducing both the number of thoughts and their intensity.

"We create success or failure on the course primarily by our thoughts." -Gary Player.

Tyler too could have used the 3-Ps after any one of his shots. After his terrible tee shot, his subconscious narrative was on fire. It is no way to start a round. When he found his ball, his 3-Ps could have been:

1. It's a par-five. I will put this next shot there to give me a good look at the flag.
2. I'm going to look at my Yellow card at my best recovery shot.
3. I'm going to make my pre-shot routine a little slower.

From the earlier chapters, you know positive and negative experiences and their commentaries do not carry the same chemical and cognitive value. It takes five positive experiences to dilute one negative experience, on average. Mark, Tyler, and yourself do not have time for five good things to miraculously happen before their next shot. Using the 3-Ps after each shot allows the neuropathways to shift so that the default negative monologues keep all future agnostic scores (surprise numbers) below 5. This will reduce the one-shot cost down the road and perhaps eliminate it entirely.

Game Day Tool 5: T&E – Talk with Eyes

When in your pre-shot routine and over a shot, you have consciously decided what it is you want to do. You want to hit the ball "there," wherever there is. This is usually the extent of the conscious command. This is not wrong and much better than not having any conscious decision of what you want to do. Frankly, though, I hardly know anyone that does not make a decision of what they want to do over a ball. Whether they can execute on that command or not is another story.

Not all conscious commands are equal. Some conscious commands can easily be infiltrated by the subconscious, such as the "Don't go left" example shared earlier. In other words, **the stronger the conscious command, the less the subconscious can do its thing.**

The strongest conscious command is what I simply call "talking with eyes" (acronym T&E). I am aware 'T&E' is not 'TWE,' but I have found it easier for golfers to remember 'T&E' than 'TWE'. Consider the different commands below over the same shot:

1. Conscious Command: I want to hit on the right side of fairway.
2. T&E Command: I want the ball to be left of that bunker, past that mound, and let the wind move it more left.

The neurological scan over these two commands are quite different. T&E command, because it is using a sense (eyes) to describe the target or ball flight, creates lower frequency brain waves than the generic command. It is because the eyes were involved in the command more purposefully, and as you know, senses suppress the subconscious. This is because the subconscious usually processes the past or future scenarios (source of non-agnostic) and the senses process the present moment.

Note that talking with your eyes is not quite the same as visualization. The latter, though good, is similar neurologically to the traditional command. Talking with eyes is a description of a unique and singular position on the golf course and where you want the ball to go and finish. Instead of closing your eyes to visualize, a traditional method, I recommend you leave your eyes open and verbalize what your eyes are seeing and what you want to do with the ball.

1. Conscious Command: I want to be below (left/right) of the hole.
2. T&E Command: I want the ball to finish past that rake, above the fringe where the shadow of the flag is. I need to flight it towards that cloud.

The margin of error as you approach the green gets smaller as you want to be closer to the hole. Both commands are good, but talking with your eyes generates more agnostic brain waves because a sense is being used to describe more attributes of the present moment, subduing the subconscious desire to create a past or future narrative. T&E is a short-term 'traveling light' strategy for the brain.

All these GYRA tools will be demonstrated in the last two chapters of the book.

"The more I practice, the luckier I get." -Gary Player.

Warm Up

Without a doubt, the pre-tournament warm up requires the most change. I have been to so many tournaments at all levels of golf, juniors to tour events, walked the range up and down, observing hundreds of golfers for hours, and virtually all golfers are preparing incorrectly from a neurological perspective, from my perspective.

The purpose of a warm up should be to prepare for what you are about to do.

This simple statement is all the argument I need.

What is a golfer about to do in a competitive round of golf?

1. Compete first with self, then the course, and then the field.
2. Hit a shot only once from the same place.
3. Have a pre shot routine for every shot.
4. Every shot in competition has a desired distance, travel path, landing location, yardage, trajectory, shape.
5. Judge every shot hit in the round (subconscious narrative).
6. Have a brain that is processing infinitely more stimuli so speed and force sensors are different than on the range.
7. The same club is not used in consecutive shots (except putting).
8. The speed of swings decreases after hitting a tee shot and as you approach a green, and then increases when you go to the next tee box. There is a change in speed/force for specific shots.
9. No training aids are used when playing.
10. Your swing instructor is not going to be playing with you, telling you what to adjust.

A warm up, therefore, should reflect as close as possible the same conditions - pragmatically, logistically, emotionally, and mentally - as those where he is about to go to.

A successful warm up can be easily defined neurologically. **The first hole should feel exactly what you would normally feel like on the fifth hole.**

How does it feel on the fifth hole? By the time you get here, you know you are playing the course, you have processed four holes of emotional, mental, and golf scores (remember - GYRA plus golf scores). Why should it take this long to feel this? It means you have not warmed up properly.

"I never hit a shot, even in practice, without having a very sharp, in-focus picture of it in my head." -Jack Nicklaus

The warm up for EQ starts from the moment you enter the golf course property. Have a landmark like a gate at the entrance or the parking lot. From that moment until you leave the golf course, begin to slowly practice macro focus via your senses. Some golfers start even before that on their drive to the course by playing their favorite music in their cars or noticing clouds and trees on the drive. You can wave at other drivers or talk to your favorite person. On game day, doing nothing is actually fertilizer for the subconscious.

So, the first change in your warm up is to use the time you have to drive to the course as your emotional and mental warm up.

Remember, a conscious effort to do this is a subconscious effort to not think of something else, especially any negativity (cortisol) that might exist in your life. Doing something Green on your drive, like the EQ Diet, is both fertilizer for your conscious and concurrently inhibiting your mind wandering subconscious. You are taking control, which is what you want to do on the course.

Once you get to the course, a neuromuscular warm up is highly recommended. There are several good activation, stretch, and warm up exercises you can do. I highly recommend seeing a professional, even if it is just once, to assess what exercises are good for your body type. My physio friends often tell me that between hitting balls and a good activation/stretch, the latter should be done. I agree with them.

Always start your golf warm up with putting. Always.

If you miss your target off the tee box with your driver by three yards, you will still likely be in the fairway with only a 1 on the Agnostic score. If you miss an iron shot to the green by three yards, you are nine feet farther from the hole. If you miss a putt by three yards, well, you know, *no bueno*. The point is that accuracy is at a premium in the short game. This fact naturally activates the senses and you have to be much more accurate with putting than any other shot. Accuracy is what should be activated in the brain and the best place to start is with putting. Done only the way I will describe below, putting will set the stage for the rest of the warm up as you will now be looking at specific targets in all future shots, just as you do when actually playing. Is that not what a warm up should be?

"If there is one thing I have learned during my years as a professional, it is that the only thing consistent about golf is its inconsistency." -Jack Nicklaus

A quick point of note. I do not recommend any training aids of any kind for the entire warm up. You will not have these on the course. You can use them when you practice, on days before the tournament, but not for your pre-round warm up. I have argued with both players and tour instructors on this point and I always defer my argument to neuroscience, not on any personal bias. Their argument is what harm is there if something is used to get the feel of something you want to feel when playing? It is a legitimate question and, like any good scientist, I have to process scientific methods and logical arguments in responding.

My response is that a golfer is about 90 minutes away from their brain about to change dramatically. Fact. Every golfer is going to hit a poor shot when playing. Fact. They are going to have a brain that is not going to be objective in evaluating - without bias - the cause of that poor shot. Fact. The brain required for performance (a *resilient* one capable of constant adjustments) is the brain we want to warm up. I, therefore, conclude that mimicking this same brain, one that has to figure out what to do on its own without any instructor or training aid, is more beneficial to the golfer in preparing him or her for what he or she is going to have to do. Why not do so with the safety net of the warm up, where the consequences are not severe? Figuring it out on your own in the warm up should also achieve the objective of the first hole feeling like the fifth hole. That mental rigor is required. In a tour event, using training aids and instructors is perfectly fine, but not before Thursday's first round.

Putting Warm Up

Every part of the warm up will begin with sensory activation. Go to the spot and look out somewhere away from where you will be hitting shots. Warm up each sense in this sequence by finding five things per sense like we did in Chapter 6: Taste, Smell, Sound, Feel, and Sight.

Take only one ball and the pin sheet for the day.

- Three putts should be hit from four different locations.
- Pick the most difficult hole on the practice green, the hole with the most slope or grain. This will require maximum micro focus.
- The four different locations should be three feet from hole, five feet from hole, then nine feet, and lastly from four feet. Three putts (same ball, your own playing ball) will be hit from each spot.
- The three putts from each location should be hit using the following parameters
  - First putt is for birdie
  - Second putt (same location) is for par
  - Third putt (same location) is for bogey
- The following scenario must be emotionally and mentally created for each putt.
  - Go through the same putting pre-shot routine you will use when playing for each putt.
  - Each putt must be to an actual hole on the pin sheet. For example, you can say for the first putt, "This is for birdie on hole 7."
  - Create the similar subconscious narrative per the result. For Birdie, you can say, "I hit a perfect 9 iron and have this birdie putt on 7." For par, you can say, "I hit a good chip to here on hole 2 to save par after a bad iron shot," and for bogey you can say, "I hit a horrible tee shot, had to punch out, and lagged my putt here for bogey."

- Whether you make or miss a putt, you may not repeat that putt. For example, if you miss the birdie putt, the next cannot be a do-over of the birdie putt. That opportunity is forever lost, just like what putting in competition is.

- For every putt, give it an Agnostic number. Making a putt is not always a dot. Be honest. If you miss a putt, the first question you should ask is, what non-agnostic thought (mind wandering) caused it? Where are you on the EQ Speedometer? Then make an adjustment before the next putt. This is what you will have to do in less than 90 minutes.

It is critical to create this emotional and mental situation. I have had hundreds of conversations with golfers post-round listening to them describe a putt, made or missed. Very rarely was a putt just a putt. There was always a story behind it, usually shots that were hit to get to the putt. The subconscious records everything and narrates this. These emotions and thoughts are exactly what you will be feeling when you play. This light intensity and resiliency to make adjustment to lighten the mental luggage or get to Green is what you want to feel; and what will cause that feeling on the first tee feeling like it is the fifth hole.

End putting with grabbing five balls and putting them at some far point on the practice green where you can hit longer putts. Each of the five putts should be hit to a different hole location. Go through the normal routine for each putt.

This is all you need to do to warm up for putting. It will likely take a little longer than what you normally do, even though you will likely be hitting far fewer putts.

This warm up routine - the emotional and mental focus used, the specificity of the target, and the lack of opportunity to repeat - will activate the brain to a similar state as the brain you will have when you play. You will be surprised when, for example, you get to the 7th hole and have the same condition as what you properly simulated.

Your neuropathways will automatically generate the 3-Ps. Because you had already made adjustments between putts (if you missed putts of simulated consequence), should you need to do so when playing, it will be also much easier for the brain to go back to something it recently did.

"I think that everything is possible as long as you put your mind to it and you put the work and time into it. I think your mind really controls everything." -Michael Phelps

Short Game Warm Up: Chipping, Pitching, Bunker

Every part of the warm up will begin with sensory activation. Go to the spot and look out somewhere away from where you will be hitting shots. Warm up each sense in this sequence by finding five things per sense like we did in Chapter 6: Taste, Smell, Sound, Feel, and Sight.

The next place to go to is the short game area.

- Take only one ball and the pin sheet for the day.
- 12 shots in total should be hit from 12 different locations, no two shots should be identical.
- Pick the most difficult holes on the practice area, the hole with the most slope or grain. This will require maximum micro focus and make standard hole/shots when playing feel easier.
- Every shot should be for getting up and down birdie, par or bogey.
- The following scenario must be emotionally and mentally created for each shot.
  - o Go through the same pre-shot routine you will use when playing for each shot.
  - o Each shot must be to an actual hole on the pin sheet. For example, you can say, "This is for birdie on the par-five 7th hole."
  - o Create the similar subconscious narrative per the result. For Birdie, you can say, "I hit two good shots on this par-five and now I have a chance to get one." For par,

you can say, "I hit a poor 2ⁿᵈ shot on 8 and need to save par," and for bogey you can say, "I hit three horrible shots on 14ᵗʰ hole, need to get up and down to this back pin just to save bogey."

- Whether you hit a good or bad shot, you may not repeat that shot. Like putting, there is no do-over. That opportunity is forever lost, just like how it is in competition.

- For every short game shot, give an Agnostic number. A good shot is not always a dot. Be honest. Better to catch your mind wandering here than on the course. If you mis-hit any shot or miss your landing spot or put the wrong spin on the ball, the first question you should ask is what non-agnostic thought (mind wandering) caused it? Where are you on the EQ Speedometer? Then make an adjustment before the next shot. This is what you will have to do in less than 60 minutes.

Range Warm Up

Every part of the warm up will begin with sensory activation. Go to the spot and look out somewhere away from where you will be hitting shots. Warm up each sense in this sequence by finding five things per sense like we did in Chapter 6: Taste, Smell, Sound, Feel, and Sight.

You will need your pin sheet and range finder. You have flexibility on what clubs you want to warm up with. Generally speaking, I am aware that most prefer to start with their wedges and work their way through the bag. I am not as concerned over the clubs that you pick as much as I am concerned about the emotional and mental condition of your brain through each shot.

For full shots:

1. Every shot must have a specific yardage, trajectory and shape to a specific point picked out by your range finder. The point could be an actual marker on the range or just a specific spot.

2. Every shot must simulate a specific hole or pin on a green. You can do this by standing behind the ball and visualizing the hole. Emotionally and mentally take yourself to that hole. Use your senses to do this.

3. Go through your normal pre-shot routine, the one you will use on the course, for each shot.

4. I do not have a ball count to recommend, but I do recommend no more than 40 minutes for this session.

5. End with:

   a. Playing the first and second shots of the first three holes in sequence using the exact clubs you think you will use based on the conditions of the day.

   b. Hit three fun shots with any club. Hit a driver where the ball is never more than 10 feet off the ground, a massive slice, or in whatever way will make you feel like you can send the ball wherever you want.

As you walk to the first tee, you should feel a very alive and empowered brain. It did not matter whether you hit good or bad shots. It only mattered that you had an intention and measurable consequence to each shot, that based on the result, you made an adjustment, and now you feel like you are walking to the fifth hole.

"The person I fear the most ... is myself." -Tom Watson

Managing Warm Up Surprises

What is equally important in the warm up is to manage surprises. There are all kinds of surprises that can happen just before your round. Not managed well, and you will be Yellow or Red going to the first tee, with your mind wandering and subconscious fully talkative, which is no good. Some of the surprises were discussed in the previous chapter, but additional ones are listed below.

The brain does not like surprises. Should one of these occur, you will have rehearsed it and still have a focused warm up.

Potential Warm Up Surprises:

1. Your driver is cracked.
2. Forgetting food or hydration.
3. Finding out your tee time has changed.
4. Paired with a negative player.
5. Paired with a slow or too fast player.
6. Forgetting to pack extra balls or gloves.
7. Greens appear faster/slower than the day before.
8. You realize you are missing a club.
9. Weird cramp or other muscle issue.
10. They changed the tee boxes.

Exercise:

Make a list of 10 warm up surprises that could happen to you just before your round.

For each one, think of a solution. Then, during earlier practice rounds, purposefully induce one or more of these surprises and see if your solution would work.

1. Surprise:

   Solution:

2. Surprise:

   Solution:

3. Surprise:

   Solution:

4.	Surprise:
	Solution:
5.	Surprise:
	Solution:
6.	Surprise:
	Solution:
7.	Surprise:
	Solution:
8.	Surprise:
	Solution:
9.	Surprise:
	Solution:
10.	Surprise:
	Solution:

Remember, golf is a game of surprises. Having a plan for what you want to do is great, but you must also have a plan for all the things that can go wrong. The previous chapters have given you specific skills to now be able to effectively do both during the warm up.

"Aptitude starts with attitude." —Greg Norman

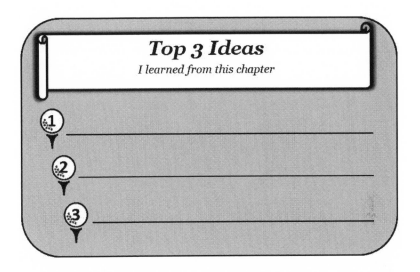

Top 3 Ideas
I learned from this chapter

1. _____
2. _____
3. _____

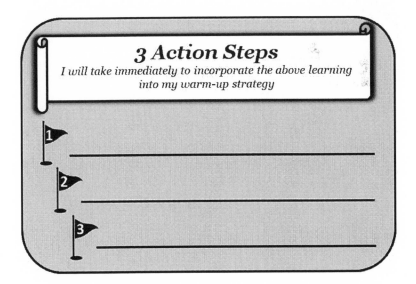

3 Action Steps
I will take immediately to incorporate the above learning into my warm-up strategy

1. _____
2. _____
3. _____

Chapter Summary

1. We need to build a GYRA golf bag with emotional and mental tools to use for different situations so that the right adjustments can be made.
2. 5-S is a tool that activates each sense with only one stimulus per sense in a sequence.
3. Slow breath, walk and talk is a tool that is a conscious effort to do these functions at a slower pace.
4. 10-2 Tension is a tool that activates (recalibrates) the sense of force, but being aware of the right tension required for a good shot.
5. 3-Ps is a tool that consciously replaces negative subconscious evaluation and judgment of a shot hit or a situation on the course.
6. T&E is a tool that allows you to "talk with eyes" so that a video image is narrated to your brain, increasing its conscious functionality to hit the shot as desired.
7. The purpose of a warm up should be to get ready to do what you are about to do.
8. Warm up must begin with putting, always, simulating what the brain will be processing on the course.
9. All shots in the warm up must be situational, recreating the emotional and cognitive state of the shot as though it is similar to a specific hole, yardage, and situation.
10. A successful warm up should be defined as playing your first hole feeling and thinking like it was your fifth hole.

Chapter 9

- *Consider how big the gap is between learning what you think you need to learn vs what you actually need to learn. Funny, the gap is always bigger when you ask an objective party.*
- *It is hard to truly comprehend that the brain is a deeply-biased vulnerable decision-making organ, which means humans are just that. We underperform largely because of not recognizing this simple truth.*
- *The starting point for personal improvement is not knowing your weaknesses ... but knowing whether your strengths can be weakened by your weaknesses.*

@izzyjustice

Making Adjustments Using the GYRA Scorecard

All this learning about our brain, about emotions and thoughts, about conscious and subconscious, about mind wandering, about traveling light, about moving the needle in the EQ speedometer, about being our own hostage negotiators, about being our own EKG machines, about all the tools, and about warming up correctly boils down to game-time performance. I have been building a case that this game of golf is largely mental and having a way to measure ourselves emotionally and mentally will lead to better performance on game day. The brain you have on game day is not the brain you have traditionally used in your practice, or warm up.

In this chapter, we will play out several game day scenarios of using the tools in the GYRA bag along with the clubs in your golf bag to help you perform at your best. There were hundreds of scenarios to pick from, but just a few were picked. The recommended adjustment will largely be the same in most of them as the real difference is in the stimulus of the moment, not so much what that does to your brain and what adjustments to make.

During the round, recall that neurologically, the most difficult shot to hit in golf is right after a bad one.

Once a shot is hit, unless it is a dot, GSGR, your mind is going to wander in its effort to make sense of the surprise. Adjustments will have to be made using the tools we have learned to make every subsequent shot agnostic, allowing those alpha and theta waves to flow.

Here are all the adjustment tools in the GYRA bag you have learned so far:

1. ACT Breathing
2. EQ Speedometer for taking your Emotional Temperature
3. Yellow and Red Cards
4. GYRA Scorecard: An Emotional and Mental Accounting system
5. Focal Thoughts: EQ, Golf, and Mental
6. Macro and Micro focus
7. EQ and Agnostic Diets one to two days before round
8. Rehearsing surprises
9. 5-S, activating senses
10. Slow breath, walk, and thought
11. 10-2 Tension
12. 3-Ps
13. T&E, talk with eyes
14. Neurological warm up

You now have 14 GYRA tools to go with 14 golf clubs! Each one of these GYRA tools is based entirely on neuroscience, not on any philosophy or individual person. It is simply what your brain will respond to.

"It isn't the mountains ahead to climb that wear you out; it's the pebble in your shoe." -Muhammad Ali

Let us go back to the first hole for Mark and Tyler, the par-five where they both scored par, and analyze their shots and recommended adjustments using the GYRA cards:

Mark's Shots	A Score	GYRA Adjustment
Good Drive	•	Macro Focus, EQ Focal Thought
Good Shot; just off green	2	Ab Breath, 3-Ps, 5-S, Yellow card of best chip, T&E
Chip lip-out	4	Take EQ Temp., EQ Focal Thought, Micro focus, Ab Breath, Slow walk/talk, 3-Ps, T&E, and 5-S while Tyler putts
Missed Putt	8	EQ Temp is likely Red having both missed easy putt and watching Tyler make long putt. Walk to second tee box should review Red Card, Taking 10-2 Tension on grip before next tee shot, and slow walk/talk.

Mark did not use any GYRA tools when playing. The adjustments are tools he could have used. He probably did not even know the negative impact of what transpired on the green. His mistake was that he did not realize:

1. The mental cost of his chip lipping out.
2. The mental cost of watching Tyler drain his long putt.

Mark's brain had no choice but to observe these two events. As such, his brain had to process both. The stimuli of these two events does not evaporate into thin air. The brain was processing both while he was going through his routine for a simple putt. His subconscious was active, creating new brain waves of higher frequencies which are largely, if not entirely, responsible for him missing the tap-in birdie. The latter was a simple putt he had made countless times. It was not a golf or technique issue; it was an emotional and mental one. He simply did not know what his brain was doing.

Note that this was the first hole, not the 18th. He has 17 holes to go and his brain has recorded it all. The "8" surprise of the missed birdie putt will cost him, according to my research, a full shot somewhere on those remaining holes especially if anything similar to what happened on the first hole were to happen again. If Tyler is away and drains another putt while Mark is closer, Mark's subconscious will do exactly what it is designed to do. It needs to evaluate Tyler's putt and it will do so against the most recent memory of a similar situation, what happened on the first hole. This does not mean that Mark will miss that putt. It does mean that the probability of Mark making the putt has gone down. If Mark misses the putt, he will likely do what I see so many golfers do: he will increase his putting practice time, change his putter, or change his putting grip, not knowing that this would be fixing the wrong problem.

Tyler's Shots	A Score	GYRA Adjustment
Driver into woods	9	Slow Ab breath, walk and talk, 3-Ps, T&E, micro focus on next shot
Punch out	4	Ab Breath, 3-Ps, T&E, Macro focus, EQ Focal Thought
Third shot into greenside bunker	4	Mental/Golf Focal Thought for bunker play, Micro focus, Ab Breath, T&E, Slow walk/talk, 5-S while Mark chips
Poor bunker shot to 15 feet	8	Slow walk, Ab Breath, Red card, should review Red Card, Take 10-2 Tension and T&E on grip before putt. Putt was a dot.

Tyler's brain and Mark's brain could not have been in more different places on this hole even though they played the same hole. The shock of a poor drive, especially for the first shot of the day, had a high Agnostic number. A good neurological warm up would not have guaranteed a good tee shot, but it would have reduced the probability that a poor shot would have been hit, and if hit, he would have processed in his warm up in a way that would have reduced his mind wandering on the course. You can see how his next three shots were all poor. A good EQ and mental diet in the preceding days where he had rehearsed the surprise of a poor first shot might have reduced the mind wandering and subconscious chatter.

Any one of the GYRA tools could have helped reduce his subconscious. He still made the big putt and saved par, but the cost of this first hole on his subsequent holes was much higher even though he likely would be Yellow, not Red like Mark, going to the next hole. Had Tyler made any of the GYRA adjustments recommended, the probability that his subsequent shots would have been better would have gone up and the overall cost of the hole would have been lower. Should Tyler use no GYRA tools, the probability that he will underperform in the rest of the round goes up. No professional athlete wants this. No competitive athlete wants this.

If you recall my good friend Heather Gollnick's write up when she saw her daughter and mother-in-law in wheelchairs as she was getting ready to give up in the Ironman, those "super Green" stimuli, spurred her to her win. She was lucky that she saw them at that moment. And good for her. But she got lucky with those stimuli. The GYRA tools take luck out of performance to allow you to perform at your best because you can induce the right stimulus at the right time on your own.

Here is an actual description, from the 2019 NGJA 12-13 age group National Champion, of some GYRA tools that were used to make adjustments in one of his tournaments, in his own words.

SCENARIO – Poor start to round:

Final Round of a tournament: I started the day off with a mental mistake on the first tee as I did not have a T to tee up my ball when it was my turn to tee off. I quickly ran over to my bag to get a tee, then ran back which caused me to be all over the place with my mind. I ended up hitting a straight pull left that hit a branch 50 yards ahead of the tee box and the ball came straight down. I proceeded to play rushed the entire hole, hitting a good third shot that got an awful bounce and went just out of bounds. This constant rush affected not only my long game, but also my short game, with me 3 putting as well. This led me to make a 9 on the first hole of the tournament (par 5). After the hole was over, I knew I was in nuclear red and had to do many things to get back to green. I first started using my ACT breathing technique and taking long slow sips of water, both to slow my heart rate down. Secondly, I pulled my nuclear red card out and picked out the best memory on it, playing with my dog Russ. I read the card slowly, while I closed my eyes and tried to take myself back to that moment in my mind. After those techniques and extra micro focus, I was fully back in green and ready to play the next shots. I proceeded to play the next 6 holes in +2, which was not awful considering that I made a 9 on the first hole. However, on hole eight I made a 30-foot breaking birdie putt that gave me the confidence I needed to get my round going. After feeling good from the last hole, I hit my tee shot on the par 3 ninth hole over water to 2 feet after spinning it back 6 feet. I caught fire after that, birding holes 14, 15, and 16. I won my age division!

-Hunter J.

What you read in Hunter's words was that he had a language (GYRA Tools) to properly diagnose what happened. He knew he was Red. He knew he was not Agnostic. This helped him be his own sports psychologist and make adjustments. His thinking about his beloved dog Russ subdued his subconscious. His competition after making a 9 on the first hole was himself, not the course or the field or his swing. His recognition of this was key to his win. I am sharing this to demonstrate that these emotional and mental skills are not difficult to learn. If a 13-year old can do it, anyone can. I have intentionally designed the scorecard and tools to be simple for everyone to use.

Potential Round Surprises

As in the previous chapter, it is worth making a list of all the surprises that could potentially happen during your round. Here are some common ones:

1. Out of bounds shot.
2. Fan or other noise during your shot.
3. Forgetting your hydration and nutrition.
4. Unexpected winds or other weather.
5. Duped into keeping pace with other players; abandoning your strategy.
6. A talkative or slow playing partner.
7. Being put on the clock.
8. Getting stung by a bee.
9. Delayed starting time.
10. Good Shot Bad Result, Bad Shot Good Result, Bad Shot Bad Result.

"The man who views the world at 50 the same as he did at 20 has wasted 30 years of his life." – Muhammed Ali

Each one of these not managed using a GYRA tool is going to be expensive emotionally and mentally, resulting in strokes lost.

This is a good time to review the examples given in Chapter 1 before proceeding with the exercise below. Every one of those stories became stories because nothing was done emotionally and mentally. There was no accounting system that the player or caddie could have used to know what to do, the way Hunter described. Imagine if all the stories in Chapter 1 would even exist had GYRA tools been used.

Exercise:

Make a list of 10 common surprises that could happen to you or have happened to you in your round.

For each one, think of a solution that includes GYRA tools. Then, during practice, purposefully induce one or more of these surprises and see if your solution would work.

1.	Surprise:	
	Solution:	
2.	Surprise:	
	Solution:	
3.	Surprise:	
	Solution:	
4.	Surprise:	
	Solution:	
5.	Surprise:	
	Solution:	
6.	Surprise:	
	Solution:	
7.	Surprise:	

	Solution:																				
8.	Surprise:
	Solution:
9.	Surprise:
	Solution:
10.	Surprise:
	Solution:

"I had to take a couple of deep breaths on the 17ᵗʰ after we squared the match because emotions were so high." -Sergio Garcia, 2016 Ryder Cup

Take a look at your story in Chapter 1 where you underperformed. Could a golf EQ, and mental strategy like this have helped you?

Here again is an actual completed GYRA card from Chapter 5.

HOLE	1	2	3	4	5	6	7	8	9	OUT	10	11	12	13	14	15	16	17	18	IN	TOTAL
YARDAGE	436	176	451	608	213	410	595	192	452	3533	431	564	239	382	439	180	381	661	460	3737	7270
PAR	4	3	4	5	3	4	5	3	4	35	4	5	3	4	4	3	4	5	4	36	71
ACTUAL SCORE	5	3	4	4	2	3	5	3	3	32	4	4	3	3	3	4	3	5	5	34	
G				x	x	x							x	x	x						
Y		x	x				x				x	x				x	x	x	x		
R	x							x	x												
A																					

Figure 13. GYRA Scorecard: Completed

I picked this GYRA scorecard from hundreds because it was a great example of scoring well despite not hitting many good shots. Mr. Nicklaus said he only hit one pure shot a round. The golfer who completed this card had only 7 dots (GSGR) the entire round and shot 66.

Here are some additional data points that will give more context to what happened before the round even begun for her.

1. The golfer's mom, whom she is very close to, was sick. She had been worried about her mom in the days leading to this tournament. This made it difficult to focus, increased mind wandering, and she knew even during her practice rounds that she was not agnostic.
2. She did not sleep well both nights prior to the round. She felt physically tired during this round.
3. Her warm up was terrible. She could not find the discipline to follow the routine we had worked on.

You can see how her brain, not having a full positive EQ Tank and not having followed any EQ or Agnostic Diet, compromised both her practice and warm up sessions. It should be no shock that her surprise numbers on the first hole were so high.

She told us that when she wrote her Agnostic numbers on her GYRA scorecard, she felt she knew what to do. The numbers she wrote were truthful, and it led to her beginning to make adjustments. After the first hole, she took out her yardage book. As part of her Red card, she had a picture of her and her mom from when she was a little girl. It is one of her favorite pictures. She said a thought suddenly came to her as she walked to the second tee box. "Why not try to fight through this and then try to tell Mom about the round so that Mom would be proud?" She used this thought from the second hole onwards as a new on-the-spot EQ Focal Thought. It became her mantra for the day.

Note that this amazingly effective thought did not just randomly appear in her brain. Looking at her Red card picture sent her neuropathways to another place. This activated positive memories that led to her new focal thought. She still did not play great on the next two holes as there were some big surprise numbers. Leveraging her focal thought, she began to use many of the GYRA tools. She started to slow her breathing and her pace of walk, she told us. She used the T&E on every shot and even though many were not GSGR, she knew they would be much worse if she did not use the GYRA tools. Based on her recognition that it was not her golf swing or anything mechanical that was off, but a very active subconscious, she made adjustments after each shot and each hole.

The only hole she told us she regretted was hole 15, the par-three where she had the plugged lie in the bunker and did the opposite of what she had done all round by doing everything faster. She said she felt rushed because her playing partners were waiting on her. It was not the bogey that bothered her, but the realization that she abandoned her GYRA tools on that hole. Because she had done well managing her chaos all round, she was not Red as she was after hole one. On the next hole, she committed to using her Yellow card and before each of the three shots she hit, she took herself to the best shot she hit with the club she was going to use and made birdie.

You may be wondering what happened on the last hole where she made bogey with some high Agnostic numbers. She told us hole 17 was the most expensive hole of the round even though she made par. She had begun to feel very physically tired and mentally drained especially after the comeback birdie on 16. Her shots were not bad but nowhere near what she was trying to do with the ball. She used 5-S several times to feel present, to be in that moment and when she saved par, she said she was about to physically just fall down. Like a marathoner on mile 25 of the run with a mile to go, and the finish line clearly in sight, she felt like she just wanted the round to be over with and had begun to again lose focus, finding it harder to macro or micro focus.

I asked her why she gave herself a Yellow EQ reading after the 18th hole. She said, "I knew I was not Agnostic but I actually was smiling because I couldn't wait to call Mom and tell her how awesome I fought to get the best out of myself when I did not have it today. I knew my telling her about how I adjusted so many times would make her smile!"

She said that this was a 75-round that she turned into a 66 using the GYRA tools.

"To control your nerves, you must have a positive thought in your mind." -Byron Nelson

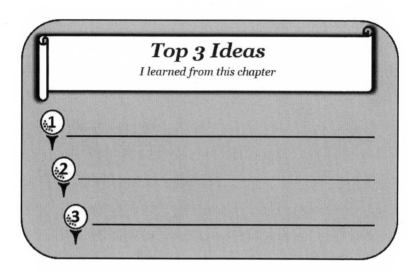

Top 3 Ideas
I learned from this chapter

1 _____

2 _____

3 _____

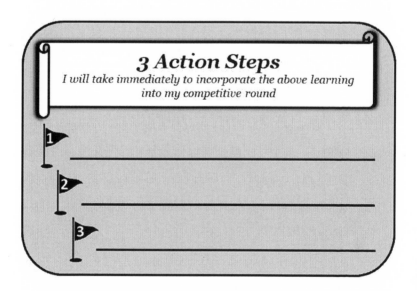

3 Action Steps
I will take immediately to incorporate the above learning into my competitive round

1 _____

2 _____

3 _____

Chapter Summary

1. Golf is a game of mistakes. Making adjustments after each one so that emotions and thoughts are being actively nurtured to be Green/Agnostic is a major golf competency.
2. Begin to adopt the 14 GYRA tools in your bag, each to use for specific situations, after shots, and between holes.
3. Proper self-diagnosis using the GYRA system will allow you to make the right adjustments.
4. If a 13-year-old can learn this, you can, too.
5. Your golf score will reflect less your golf skills and more your ability to recover from your worst shot.

Chapter 10

- *Everyone tells me they like to learn. No one tells me they like to change.*
- *Emotional malnourishment can never be cured by a purchase, ever. Being authentic and having authentic relationships can. Just one of the latter is more nourishing than 100 purchases. Reduce purchases so you have fewer masks to authenticity.*
- *Don't measure the success of your year solely by what you accomplished. Consider how many new friends you made, how many people you helped, how much you've grown & how many bad habits you broke away from.*

@izzyjustice

Q School with GYRA

In this last chapter, while thinking of ways to "put it all together" for you, I thought a powerful way would be to have a golfer in arguably one of the most stressful scenarios, Qualifying School, chronicle the entire week. Whether you are a junior, collegiate player, an amateur, or a professional; and whether you are playing a one-day tournament or a four-day tournament, you should be able to see yourself somewhere in this very honest sharing by Matt Ryan, a KFT Tour player. Very little editing was done intentionally so that his raw story could be relatable to anyone.

Matt Ryan – Second Stage Q School

Most professional golfers looking to gain membership to the Korn Ferry Tour and eventually on to the PGA Tour have to go through Korn Ferry Tour (KFT) Qualifying, also known as "Q-School." KFT Qualifying consists of four stages starting in September and running through December. At each stage, there are a pre-determined number of players that will advance to the next stage based on the total field size for their respective qualifying sites. For a player to earn Korn Ferry Tour status, he must advance to the Final Stage of KFT Qualifying in December.

Every qualifying stage gets more difficult because, for the most part, the better players advance, as well as many players being exempt into deeper stages of qualifying. Second Stage, which takes place in November at four different locations across the country, is where PGA Tour winners from years past and Korn Ferry Tour players who lost their full status from the previous year will enter. At the Final Stage, there will be more former PGA Tour winners and Korn Ferry Tour winners exempt to play four rounds of golf in Orlando, FL, for playing privileges the following year.

Anytime "Q-School" is mentioned in the golf world, you will hear people talk about how much pressure is involved. If you can interpret pressure to mean "there are too many thoughts in your head and most of them are negative," then you can acknowledge and replace those thoughts with GYRA tools. In other words, you will be attempting to limit your subconscious and mind wandering as much as you can.

The hardest part of the KFT Qualifying stages is that the subconscious is extremely active. This is what every player prepares for all year. You know if you do not get through one of the stages, your year is over and you're back to playing mini tours, not any closer to reaching your dream. Basically, as a professional golfer, every fall season you are competing to earn your job for the following year.

Due to the ramifications of not qualifying, every round feels like the final round of a golf tournament while in contention. In a final round, the end of the tournament is near, with only 18 holes left; therefore, your subconscious is going to be more active. "I want to win." "I want to finish top 10." "Where does this put me on the money list?" Every shot feels like it counts that much more. Usually, when you're in contention going into a final round, you have played great golf. At Q-School, you may be in 20th place, not playing that great, and you have to summon the courage to go out there and shoot a low number so you can "survive and advance." KFT Qualifying is a breeding ground for the subconscious to take over and put doubt into your mind every step of the way, causing your brain to wander like it never has before. You cannot simulate the "pressure" at Q-School.

In November of 2019, I drove from Charlotte, NC, down to Brooksville, FL, for the Second Stage of KFT Qualifying. I was exempt to Second Stage based on how I had performed up to that point on PGA Tour Latino America; the top 25 on the Order of Merit were exempt to Second Stage and I was in that group. Getting exempt to any stage of KFT Qualifying is always a huge bonus and moves you that much closer to ending the year as a Korn Ferry tour member.

Saturday

The Second Stage is played from Tuesday to Friday, so I drove down to Brooksville, FL, on Saturday, which takes about nine and a half hours. Just like the way I use Mondays for most tournament weeks, I treated that Saturday as a travel day. This is when my tournament week starts, three days before the first tournament round. This is all part of my EQ Diet, which I use throughout the week to limit surprises and actively seek out activities to make me Green.

On travel days, I script a lot of macro focus. In this case, I planned my drive on the way from Charlotte, NC, to Brooksville, FL. I packed food so everything I ate I was in control of. In hours one and two, I settled into my drive with a playlist of new songs that I like. Hour three was an "observing hour." My phone was off for the entire hour, and for the first 30 minutes, I read every single sign posted along the highway and recognized the make and model of every single car on the road.

The second half hour I used for seeing as many colors as I could find in the scenery around me; green trees, brown trunks, blue sky, white clouds, black road, yellow lines, etc. During hours four and five, I made phone calls to people I wanted to get in touch with. Before planning who I called, I made sure that the people I talk to would fill my EQ tank and not deplete any of it.

Hours six and seven I turned on some podcasts, or educational TED Talks. For the 30 minutes after the podcasts, I tried to be very conscious about what I was feeling. I did a slow body scan, feeling the steering wheel, my butt in the seat, the pedal I had my foot on, moved my hand to a water bottle, etc. This activated my senses, which I knew I would need during the tournament. With an hour and a half left on my drive, I gave myself some free time for an hour to do whatever I wanted to do. The last 30 minutes, I went back to recognizing my surroundings. I did this because when I enter the course property I wanted to feel completely immersed in my arena.

My travel day is also a scouting day at the course. I find out where the bathrooms are, where the range is, where the putting green is, where the chipping green is, where tees one and 10 are, my route to the golf course, where the gym is and whether or not I'll be able to work out for the week. I don't like to be searching for places or things when I show up to play and practice on Tuesdays. When it comes to all of the grunt work on Mondays, any tournament site you have been to in previous years is a bit easier because you won't have to discover again all of the things I just mentioned. This was my fifth trip to Southern Hills Plantation, which helps limit how many possible surprises there will be for the week. I successfully advanced two times at Southern Hills

Plantation out of the four trips prior. I really enjoy the golf course when I know the surrounding area quite well.

I knew where everything was located and I was staying with a wonderful family I met three years prior to this trip. I knew what my room looked like, what bathroom I would be using, where the gym would be, and what equipment I would have available. I was also very aware that hole #10 was a shuttle ride from the clubhouse. Knowing all of this and planning for it can be very useful to limiting even more surprises throughout the week. Limiting surprises reduces mind wandering, lowers agnostic numbers, and allows me to use other GYRA tools to be Green and Agnostic.

Sunday

Sunday of that week I treat as I do Tuesdays in a normal tournament week. The course during KFT Qualifying is not available to play until 12:00 pm. Therefore, I planned accordingly. I woke up at 7am and had a "slow" morning, eating breakfast at 7:30am, and then I left for the gym at 8:15am. I was at the gym for about 45 minutes to get in a good rotational and stretching workout. I also did some golf specific workouts just to loosen my body up after the long drive the day before.

After the gym, I went back to the house, ate again, and left for the course, arriving at 10am. Having two days before the start of the tournament, I used that day to check all of my basics. I used my putting tools to check my putt alignment and ball position. I also checked my alignment and ball position on the range. THIS IS THE LAST DAY I DO ANYTHING MECHANICAL.

I love playing nine holes the couple of days before tournament weeks. My plan was to play nine on Sunday and nine on Monday with no particular plan to play with anyone. Not committing to playing with anyone affords me the luxury to feel more relaxed and in control with my own time. I walked to the first tee at 12:00 pm and along the way I was asked by Trevor Cone from Concord, NC, to play together. Trevor is a great guy and a fantastic player. We play together quite a bit in Charlotte and we have also played many practice rounds throughout the years together. Again, little things like this create even fewer surprises. KFT qualifying is no place to introduce new things to my golf world.

The biggest reason for me limiting most practice rounds (outside of pro-ams) to nine holes is to get some macro focus going on specific holes at specific moments. Dr. Justice has even recommended taking holes off during practice rounds to connect with something intimately on the hole without any golf attachment to it. For example, in some other tournament practice round, I will not play every third hole but go to all the places my ball would be on those holes and just visualize golf shots without hitting any. It's amazing to me how every time I am on a hole where I did this, I just naturally smile remembering what I did.

Although I did not do that during Second Stage, I was very conscious of how I was feeling on particular holes and keeping notes in my yardage book about particular things that would make me Green and Agnostic. One of the things I often write near the tee boxes in my yardage book is, "enjoy the starter on the first tee." I write this to make sure when I head to the first tee, I really appreciate the person's time to be out there with us all day. I want volunteers to know that I am happy to be there and thankful to be playing a sport I love.

At Southern Hills Plantation the beauty is quite endless. Green grass, big live oak trees with Spanish moss hanging down, lakes, native grass, and a beautiful clubhouse. There is a way to connect with every hole if you are looking for it. There is a lake about 30 yards behind the first green and there are usually Sandhill Cranes hanging around. So, I took out my yardage book and wrote at the top (behind the green) "Sandhill Cranes." It's a weird feeling how these non-golf related notes can get me overly excited to play the holes. I look forward to seeing all of the points of interest I have personally picked out to enjoy every hole.

From holes #3 to #8, it is nearly impossible to not pay attention to the live oaks with Spanish moss hanging from them. Live oaks are most certainly my favorite tree. I grew up in the Santa Clarita Valley in Southern California, where big live oaks with dark brown trunks and dark green leaves sit on the surrounding hills in long stretches of yellow native grass. I also got married in Savannah, Georgia, where live oaks with hanging Spanish moss have become synonymous with the beautiful parks spaced throughout the city. It is safe to say that live oaks take my brain to nothing but Green moments in my life, and therefore I try to SEE each one that I walk by when playing Southern Hills.

After my nine holes were over, I went to the driving range. On the range, I put an alignment stick down and went through each shot I hit on the front nine, hitting to specific yardages. After the range, I headed to the chipping green where I used green, yellow, and red rings to help visualize chipping and pitching with different trajectories. With each chip I hit, I tried to imagine I was on one of the holes chipping to a specific pin. Then I went back to the putting green where I checked my alignment and ball position one last time. After that I played a putting game called "3-6-9," where I tried to make every putt I could from 3 feet, 6 feet, and 9 feet, 18 putts in total. By the time all of this was over, it was about 4:00 pm and I headed back to the house.

For the late afternoons and early evenings, I had a plan as well. I always get books that are not golf related to read during tournament weeks. That week I had with me my favorite book, "Gates of Fire" by Steven Pressfield, which I read for about an hour before dinner. The lovely couple that I stay with, Bruce and Annie, offered to make dinner that night and we ate at 6:30 pm. I remember what time we ate so distinctly because I know that Bruce and Annie love to watch Jeopardy!, which airs at 7:30pm. Every night that week I watched Jeopardy! with them, then I would head off to bed.

Before laying down in bed, I made a list on a sheet of paper with two columns, Positive & Negative. On this list I tracked everything that happened during the day. Things I really enjoyed and want to do more of, and as well as things I did not like and what I want do to less of. This helps me separate my Green and Red experiences throughout the day and allows me to focus on how to be better tomorrow. When I am done making the list, I write down two sentences— "Tomorrow I will be a better golfer because..." and "Tomorrow I will be a better person because..." Dr. Justice always wants me to go to bed with an empowered brain.

Monday

Again, Monday of a Q-School week is the same as a Wednesday in a normal tournament week. I will not have any more than four hours of golf the day before a tournament unless I am in a pro-am. When I am not in a pro-am, I love getting all of my work in early. Wednesday is all about emotionally and mentally resting so I can be completely filled up for the days that follow. I have a specific EQ Diet plan for this day.

I went to the course at 6:45am. My plan was to warm up, play nine holes, practice, and leave. When I first arrived, I walked to the putting green and found a good spot to sit down and activate my five senses (5-S). When doing this, I find myself calming and feeling more agnostic.

After that, I hit five putts. I hit two putts from three to five feet, creating a live video for the putt, rolling in the exact pace I would like to see the ball go in with MY perfect speed. I want to feel the speed in my head and activating my senses before helps me do this. I hit two five sensations with each sense, in a specific order — smell, taste, hear, feel, and see. I do it in this specific order because I leave the strongest senses for the end to allow myself to really engage with my sense of smell and taste first. Lastly, I find one NEW stimulant for each sense going in the same putts from 12 feet.

Lastly, I hit one lag putt creating a live video focusing on the target. Now that putting was done, before I played, I went to the range and hit MAYBE 20 balls. I was quite literally just warming up to go play. I still created a scenario in my head for shots I will hit on the back nine and hit balls to a specific target with a certain distance in mind. After that, I hopped on the five-minute shuttle ride to the 10th tee.

Very similarly to the day before playing the front nine, I used Monday to connect with holes 10-18. The only difference was that I stayed very conscious of the goal that day; emotional and mental rest, which really means keep low frequency thoughts and observations. I marked down the wildflowers that grow near the lake behind #10 tee box and made a point to notice them every day before and after I hit my tee shot. #11 and #12 have a pretty stream that lines the left sides of both holes. Once you hit numbers 14, 15, and 16 at Southern Hills Plantation, there are TONS of the live oaks with Spanish moss hanging. I made plenty of notes in my yardage book about which trees to look at in particular. On #17, a mid-length par-three, there is a small bridge you cross over and a lake to the left. More times than not on sunny days, an alligator or two will be out on the banks. I love watching animals while I am playing golf, so I made a note of that in my yardage book as well. Again, all of these points of interest I am writing down in my book have to do with me creating some sort of personal attachment to the holes that I play; things which will help me stay Green and Agnostic.

After playing, I started a practice session that only lasted an hour and a half. I went to the driving range for some EQ practice. Before I hit balls, I closed my eyes and started to do the 5S. Meaning I engaged my senses the same as I did in the morning next to the putting green, but only one stimulant for each sense. While I hit balls, I was very conscious of my subconscious thoughts, making sure for every single shot that I hit, I was striving to be 100% Agnostic.

I picked an exact trajectory and distance I wanted to hit the ball and what green (hole on course) I might be hitting into. Before stepping into the shot, I created a moving picture of the ball's trajectory by using my sight and feel senses. I never hit a shot without having a clear picture. My only objective on the range is to be overly prepared for the days to follow. After each shot, I asked myself if it deserved a "dot." Was it a GSGR? Was it exactly how it was in the picture before the shot? If it was not, then I used another GYRA tool. Just like I do in all tournament rounds, if the shot I hit is over a "3" I go to my GYRA tools and pick one to do before my next shot. Those tools include relaxing my upper body and/or lower body, ACT breathing, 10-2, 3Ps, or stopping and doing another five senses.

After the range, I went to the chipping green to work on the short game. I hit 15 shots, with my own ball of course, and my goal is to make every shot go in hole. By doing this, I took time for each shot in the same manner I was going to do it in the tournament. With the short game, I do everything in my power to lock into my moving picture exactly how the ball will be traveling from landing spot to the hole. Similar to the driving range, I took note after each shot on whether or not it was a "dot." If it was not, I did a quick 5, or any number of my GYRA tools before even starting the process of the next chip. After chipping, I did the same process with my bunker play, hitting five shots all from different lies and all to different holes.

Lastly, and in my opinion most importantly, I went to the putting green. I say most important because the putting green is where the most emotional energy can be gained or lost during the week of a tournament. Once again, before hitting any putts, I closed my eyes and did a quick 5S. I hit 30 putts in total using one ball, and I always putt from a different spot on the green. The first 20 putts were all putts from 12 feet, and in mixing up the distances from 3 feet, 6 feet, 9 feet, and 12 feet. Just like every other facet of the game, I created a picture. It is key to hold that picture throughout the process of hitting a putt. Quite literally seeing and feeling the picture with my senses, not my thoughts. The last 10 putts I hit were long range. All were hit from different places on the green.

To summarize my practice the day before a tournament, it is always about GYRA and never about anything that has to do with the mechanics of golf.

Once practice was all finished it was 12:00 pm. Continuing with my EQ Diet plan for the day, I went to the gym to get a workout in. I love feeling athletic during golf weeks. This is definitely something that helps fill up my EQ tank. After the gym I went to the house, showered, and got my bag ready for the next day. While getting my bag ready the days before a tournament, I always clean my clubs and my grips. It is something I have done since I was a kid when I first started playing golf. My Dad always used to wash his clubs and say, "If you take care of your clubs, your clubs will take care of you." I know for a fact that washing my clubs has become a bit nostalgic for me. There is not a moment that goes by when I get my bag ready for the next day that I do not think about my Dad. He had an incredible impact on me growing up as an athlete and I am thankful for him every day. Anyway, one of the most important things I did that day was lay down for an hour and close my eyes. I did not fall asleep and had no intention to. All I wanted to do was close my eyes to give them a break from processing the world around me. I thought about my potential positive-negative list for that evening, I tuned in with all of my senses and just relaxed.

At 4:00 pm, I sat down in my room and watched "Remember the Titans" before meeting some friends for dinner. I have a list of my favorite movies and I try to watch at least one during my tournament weeks. I met Trevor Cone, Will Gordon, and Tee-K Kelly for dinner at Carrabba's Italian Grill that evening. All three guys I get along with very well, they are all great players, and I knew the dinner would provide a lot of good, non-golf conversation and laughter. I am very aware of who I surround myself with, especially the night before the biggest tournament of the year. The last thing I want to do is surround myself with people that could make me Yellow or Red. Once dinner was over, I drove home and listened to a playlist of some of my favorite songs that I made specifically for that week. I watched an episode of

"The Office", which is one of my favorite TV shows, wrote down my positive and negative list for the day, and was in bed by 9:00 pm.

Tuesday

The morning of the first round is always an amazing feeling, I love the excitement I feel when getting ready in the morning. It's the first day that I get to put all the hard work into tournament play. When I get up, the first thing I do is sit on the edge of the bed and do some ACT breathing. After ACT breathing, I keep my eyes closed and go through my five senses. If I have any thoughts about golf, I bring them right back to the current moment I am in by activating a sense. While showering I feel the water, while brushing my teeth I taste the toothpaste, and while getting dressed I feel everything I touch. I get dressed slowly and intentionally. I tell myself I'm already starting my round warm up.

I also love making breakfast. I do everything I can to smell everything I make and to taste every single bite. After eating, I smell and feel every moment of putting on my sunscreen. Just before I leave, I do a quick warm up of the body which includes leg swings, rotational and stability exercises, and some fast step swings with the other end of my four iron. Due to my drive only being three minutes, I have one song queued up, "There Will Be Time" by Mumford & Sons. I chose this song because it is very special to my wife and I, and it makes me incredibly Green! I tell myself, if I can control all this in my life, I can control anything that can happen on the course.

I arrive at the course an hour and 10 minutes early. My plan is always to putt for 15 minutes one hour prior to teeing off. After putting, I chip for 10 minutes, I hit balls for 25 minutes, and then I head to the tee, getting there five to 10 minutes prior to my tee time. While sitting or kneeling next to the putting green, I go through each one of my five senses finding five things for each one, then I go through each sense with a quick 5S. After that, I start putting and do everything very similarly to my Monday putting practice. I am extremely aware of my non agnostic thoughts and hitting every putt with the intent to mark a dot.

Before going to the chipping green, I hit three right to left breaking putts in a row from 4 feet to 6 feet. The first of three putts is for birdie. I quite literally tell myself, "I hit a great drive on the first hole and then a solid GW to 4 feet and now I have this birdie putt." Dr. Justice is right in that this is most identical to what my head will be processing in actual play. My only goal is to be as Agnostic as possible, seeing and feeling the energy of the pace on the ball.

The second and third putts I hit from the same exact spot with the only difference being that the second putt is for par and the third putt is for bogey. For both putts, I created a scenario of how I ended up with the 4-foot putt just like I did for the first one. The reason I did this is because after hitting the first putt I knew exactly what the putt does, therefore the only way I can miss the putts for par and bogey is if I am not Agnostic. If I miss one, I go through the same exact process I would go through on the course. I acknowledged and replaced my non-Agnostic thought and used one of my GYRA tools to get Agnostic.

With 45 minutes until my tee time, I hit the chipping green. I went through nearly the same chipping practice I did on Monday, focusing very heavily on creating my moving picture, and monitoring my subconscious thoughts every step of the way.

I head to the range with 35 minutes left before my tee time. I walk slow, all the while remaining in my own world. I say hello to people I know and I am friendly but that is about it. Just like putting and chipping, my range warm up is very similar to Monday's. If I feel like a shot is over a three (Agnostic Scale), I hit the shot over again. The only difference from Monday's practice session are the last five shots. My last five shots I save to hit the shots I am going to hit on holes #1 through #3. Once that is done, I head to the tee.

Like I said earlier, every single time I walk to the first tee, I do it with a smile for the volunteer that is teeing us off. I want to put smiles on other's faces. It helps me stay Green. While standing on the first tee, I put a mark down in the middle of the Yellow section on my GYRA scorecard. I like to read my Yellow card before my first shot of the day and I also get into some deep micro focus seeing or feeling 10 different things. It's an amazing sensation when I feel ready to go, so overly prepared for the mission that I have to accomplish.

Through five holes, I was two under. Up to that point I only hit one green. Needless to say, my short game was great and my EQ was on fire. I thought to myself walking to six tee, "Today feels like one of those days where I am not going to make a bogey." The very next hole, I made a three-putt bogey. In 2019, I had many bogey-free rounds and many times I would have the exact same feeling I had walking off of hole five; the difference was I did not do a good job of using GYRA tools. I know the mind wanders no matter how "in the zone" I am, but when it does, getting back to the step right in front of me is huge and I did not do that. The emotions I feel when I do something that I know is wrong are not that hard to explain. I felt embarrassed because I know what I did wrong, I am mad at myself because I've probably made the mistake before, and then I immediately "go to work" and load up the EQ.

My Dad used to say, "Son, sometimes you just gotta be tough." The difference from when I was a kid to now is that I know the right way to move forward. I immediately marked down Red on my EQ scorecard for the simple fact I know that Q School amplifies every emotion. I wanted to make sure I was on the cautious side. While walking to the seventh tee box, I used ACT breathing, I found one of the many live oak trees with Spanish moss, read my Yellow card, and drank some water. I finished two under on the front nine with a great birdie on number nine.

#10 at Southern Hills Plantation gives me the heebie jeebies. It is a 410-yard straight away par-four. There is a hazard down the right side, and if you hit it left of the fairway, it is basically an automatic lost ball. I know from years of playing it that hitting 3W or driver off the tee will get my ball down a hill in the middle of the fairway leaving a wedge in. With a wedge it's a very good birdie chance. If I miss the fairway, six is a very real possibility. Anyway, my plan was to make sure I stay Agnostic going to 10 tee and not feel rushed. I asked the shuttle driver to drop me off where they cross the street, about 80 yards away from the tee. I know if I get out and walk, I will pass right by the wildflowers and lake off the back of the tee box that I made a note of during my practice round. This creates an intimate connection to the hole. I took a look at "bunt driver" on my Yellow card. That is a shot I've had with me over the years that I hit when the pressure is on, a fairway finder if you will. I move the ball a tiny bit back in my stance, take an extra pause in transition, and stay aggressive through the ball. It causes me to "lean on the ball" just slightly and I can hit the ball extremely low with a little cut. I stepped up and striped the ball down the middle.

While the other two guys were hitting, I pulled out my "18 Stories" card (a card with positive stories/memories I prepared in advance from Dr. Justice's earlier book Golf EQ). In the GYRA scorecard, I will just put those stories in abbreviated titles in its own row at the bottom of GYRA rows and read the story I had listed, "Kickoff return for TD - nerves." I completely immersed myself in the memory.

My story was referring to the first football game I ever started in full pads my freshman year of high school. I was returning the opening kickoff and my nerves were on fire. These are good nerves, though, and the same ones I get while playing golf. I always tell people that if I didn't have nerves, I would be worried because it means I really care about what I am doing. I love that feeling. I can close my eyes and remember every moment of the play; catching the ball, every step I took, and every block that was made by my teammates. I remember crossing the goal line and all of the nerves turned to excitement, we were up 6-0.

This story takes me back to a time when I was completely Agnostic and successful at something I had only dreamt about up to that point. By the time I was done daydreaming, I was at my next shot. I used 10-2 with my PW before I hit my shot from 127 yards. I hit a beautiful abbreviated wedge to 8 feet just short and left to a back right pin. The whole way up to the green I released all tension from my upper body. Relaxing my forehead, eyes, jaw, shoulders, elbow, and hands. I was most definitely Green and very Agnostic by the time I got to my 8-foot putt. I held my picture the entire way up to stroking my putt and made it for birdie. I had executed my GYRA game plan to perfection. Dr. Justice has taught me that what I do between shots with my brain is the prep work for me to be Agnostic over a shot. I only need to be Agnostic for 10 seconds, the time over a shot and hitting it. GYRA tools are designed to get me to those 10 seconds.

The rest of the way in, I stuck to my GYRA game plan the best I could. When things are going well, I don't overdo it. I stick to the plan that I have in my GYRA scorecard and stay focused on the task at hand. I use my stories from tee box to fairway, and from fairway to green, I use one of my senses that I also have written down in my GYRA scorecard. Although I only hit 5 greens on the back nine, I shot three under with four birdies and one bogey. I shot 67 in total to get off to a good start.

I felt really good about my round on the short drive home. I felt so good about my EQ. Having not hit it very solid, I scored quite well, getting up and down 9 times out of 10. With the ability to stick to a great EQ Diet plan the few days prior to the first round, my tank was full and it showed on day one, my short game was awesome. Now I needed to fill it back up.

At the house, I focused on moving slowly, talking slowly, eating slowly, etc. I knew that naturally my mind wanted to speed up after a good round of golf and I had to work to slow it down. Staying with a host family can really be great because I can use them to completely escape from golf. They asked how I played and I responded with "67." I do not give any judgment, explanation, or narration about how the round went or what it could have been. If I did that then the conversation could go anywhere, most likely to places I don't need them to go to —— places that could potentially deplete my emotional energy.

I went out of my way to ask how their day went and what they were up to. I also told them I was ready for Jeopardy! at 7:30pm. Before dinner I opened my book that I brought, "Gates of Fire", and read for about 45 minutes. Once again, Bruce and Annie were nice enough to make dinner that evening. There are a lot of things to be thankful for in professional golf and it is very easy to be thankful when people open up their home to me and trust that I will be a good guest during one of the most important weeks of my life. Recognizing gratitude is one of many feelings I try to have after rounds of golf to help me refill my EQ tank.

After watching two episodes of "The Office", I wrote down my positive and negative list, thought about how I was going to be better the next day as a person and a golfer, and went to bed. That night while trying to fall asleep I cycled through all five senses one last time and held onto the feel of my head resting in the pillow until I fell asleep.

Wednesday

I woke up just before my alarm went off Wednesday morning. That tends to happen to me quite often. I believe when that happens it's just my body letting me know I am completely rested and ready to attack the day. To be completely honest, everything was pretty much the same as the morning before just moved up by one hour. I played a different song on the way to the course, Old Friends by Ben Rector, another song that makes me entirely Green.

I got to the course 20 minutes earlier than I did for the first round. I allotted 10 minutes for the shuttle ride from the driving range to #10. I also gave myself 10 extra minutes so I could hit a few extra wedges shots on the range. The first thing I did on the range was use something that Dr. Justice gave me to help improve my moving picture. He told me to go through my whole routine as if I was hitting a ball without actually hitting it. My only focus was on following exactly how the ball was going to travel in the air to my target with an emphasis on the last half. After a few rounds of that I started my normal tournament warm up routine. While getting a ride to hole #10, I stared at my Red card.

My Red card was a group picture of myself and my friends from Ireland after playing a round of golf at Mt. Juliet Golf Club in Kilkenny, Ireland the year before. I like for my Red cards to take me to a very specific place in time that create nothing but good brain waves. Pictures help me with that. One of my closest friends is Irish PGA Tour player Séamus Power. His friends from his hometown have become very close friends of mine over the years and our group is nicknamed "Prizebull." Gary Hurley, who plays on the Challenge Tour and was a member of the 2015 Walker Cup team, is also a member of Prizebull. Every other person in Prizebull is a member at West Waterford Golf Club in Dungarvan, Ireland. West Waterford Golf Club has become a very special place to me. The owners and its members are always sending me well wishes and their support is amazing. This picture takes me to all of those great, happy thoughts. Every time I look at it, it puts a smile on my face and I can't help but move towards being Green. That is what a Red card has to do.

In round two, I did not hit too many solid full shots. I hit some of the best short game shots I've ever hit, though. I am not quite sure why I was so poor with the long game. I know the answer is that I was not as Agnostic as I needed to be, I'm just not sure why. I felt like I was doing everything I could to get Agnostic with every ball I hit. I used all the GYRA tools I could.

Although my GYRA tools didn't seem to be helping with my long game, they definitely were with my short game. Right out of the gates on hole #10, I mis-hit a PW about 15 yards short and left to a back left pin, completely short-sided. After I hit the shot, I grabbed that same Red card and thought about Séamus and how many incredible places he gets up and down from when we play golf together. I immediately relaxed, went straight to ACT breathing and completely relaxed the lower body.

My ball was sitting on wet ground with the grass laying into me. The degree of difficulty was high. I walked up to the green and imprinted a moving picture. This shot was going to be an all-out flop shot. Holding onto that picture I hit the shot about 15ft in the air. It landed a yard onto the green and trickled out to 6ft. Before it was my turn to putt, I grabbed my glove and found five things on it to look at that I had never seen before. I rolled the putt right in the center. I remember giggling after I made the putt and thought "Séamus would have enjoyed that one."

On my 3rd hole of the day I hit my second shot about 15-20 yards right of the green. #12 is a par-five and I was going to have to hit another mega flop to have a good birdie chance. From my angle, I only had about three yards of green to work with and I was hitting the ball out of Bermuda rough. Luckily, I had a good lie to hit a super high pitch. My vision of the shot was so clear and I was feeling extremely Green. I hit another great flop shot to about one foot and walked up to tap it in for birdie.

I know when I am Green because I feel that no matter what happens on the golf course I am accepting of my poor shots and completely unfazed. I have this overwhelming sense of calm. Another great example of how my EQ work directly affected my short game was on #18, my 9th hole of the day. A 481yd par 4 with an extremely narrow green. If the wind is out of a certain direction you can have four iron into the raised green that looks about 12yds wide. With a middle left hole location, I mis-hit a 6 iron to the left of the green. Short-sided again. Looking at my EQ scorecard I put down a 6 for my Surprise number. I didn't feel Red in the slightest but I know that a 6 is a Red number. I looked at my Red card once again. Then I looked at my Yellow card and read about a pitch I made in Tijuana, Mexico earlier that year on the 18th hole to finish the round with a course record 62. I went on to hit another crazy flop shot to a tap in and went to the front nine even par, having made one birdie and one bogey on the back nine.

Every nine holes played at Second Stage feels like the back nine on a Sunday in terms of emotional energy. Every hole feels like it carries more importance than it should. My subconscious is screaming to get out and causing me not to be Agnostic. It knows that one bad hole can lead to not advancing to Final Stage and therefore not earning Korn Ferry status for the following year.

On #1 tee, I reminded myself of this and how important it was for me to stick to the work I've put all year and really poured myself into my GYRA scorecard. For a good nine holes all that mattered is that I had the discipline to be Green and Agnostic. I started off the nine holes with six straight pars. Some of those were steady, hitting the greens in regulation, and just narrowly missing some birdie putts. The other hole I missed the green in regulation and was getting up and down.

On the par five 7th for my second shot, I had 280yds to a middle, right pin. The shot played 20yds downhill and if you land the ball 10yds to 20yds short, it will run all the way to the front edge. This was a perfect two iron for me. I saw my moving picture and stepped into my shot. During my last glance at my target, I lost the picture in my head. I completely mis-hit my two iron, hitting it thin with a slice to the left. My ball ended up in a small pot bunker which was lucky because it could have easily been in the hazard that lines the entire left side of the hole.

My heart rate was extremely high at this point, because I knew I should have stepped off of my shot before I hit it. I did not have the discipline to practice my GYRA training. I knew exactly what to do, though. I immediately said out loud five positives, two more than the 3Ps! "I am a great bunker player. My ball is still in play. It's a gorgeous day. I am thankful to be playing golf for a living. I am great at getting tough up and downs." I then took a very deep breath and SLOWLY released it to lower my heart rate. I grabbed my Yellow card and read my bunker shot written down on it. I actually wrote down two bunker shots on my Yellow card that I hit earlier in the round on holes #12 and #15. I read them both while calmly walking up to the green. My bunker shot was 42yds off of firm sand. I grabbed my 50-degree GW, used 10-2, and swung it like a standard bunker shot. Sometimes shots with a higher degree of difficulty are much easier to hold onto the moving picture because you may only have one option to successfully execute the shot. Therefore, it is easier to be completely Agnostic. I ended up hitting my bunker shot to 3ft and made it for birdie.

Again, my short game absolutely shined in round two, getting up and down 10 out of 11 times. Five of those up and downs were out of green side bunkers with the longest putt being 4ft. I finished the day one under par having made two birdies and one bogey. Through two rounds I got up and down 20 out of 22 times. This has everything to do with EQ. Ultimately EQ, for me, takes discipline, and I did a great job being disciplined through two days of Second Stage.

That afternoon I went to the gym for a workout. Again, I never do anything crazy during tournament weeks like heavy lifting or more than an hour at the gym. I did another full body workout with a lot of functional movement exercises. As a reminder, the gym, for me, works as something to help me refill my EQ tank for the next day. The second round was extremely draining, expensive in the emotional sense, and I could feel it.

Back at the house, I laid down and took a 20-minute nap. After that, it was much of the same routine, taking some time to rest my eyes and get off of my feet. I read my book for about an hour. When I pick up that book, I get completely immersed in it which is a great escape from the magnitude of the Q School week. After that, it was much of the same. Dinner with Bruce and Annie, Jeopardy!, my positive and negative list, an episode of The Office, and then bed by 9:30pm.

Thursday

I was very excited for Thursday. Up until that point, I carried my own bag for the first two days, but today my best friend Steven Atwood was driving up from St. Petersburg, FL, to caddie for me. Steven and I met at College of The Canyons in 2004, where we played one year of Junior College golf together. From the first day we met we were best friends. Having him on the bag was going to be great.

Steven has caddied for me several times over the years. More specifically, he caddied for me at Southern Hills Plantation in 2013, where I shot 17 under and medaled for Second Stage of Korn Ferry Tour Qualifying. Steven also caddied for me at Final Stage of Korn Ferry Tour Qualifying in 2017 where I shot 65-61 in Chandler, AZ, on the weekend to earn my full card for 2018. Steven refers to our rounds of golf together when he is on the bag as "just two friends walking in the park."

After studying under Dr. Justice, I have realized how important it is to "escape" from golf to give your brain a rest throughout the day. In other words, 18 Stories. Steven and I always do a great job reminiscing and telling stories that make us Green when we're together just because we love to catch up. I never realized what a major contribution that was to playing good golf. Furthermore, not only does Steven always express how much faith he has in me as a golfer, he knows me on a personal level better than anyone else in the world with the exception of my wife, Rachel. Therefore, Steven can easily judge whether or not I am

Green, Yellow, or Red at all times. I just felt that today was going to be an amazing day.

The only other thing I changed for Thursday was my Red card. I like to alternate my Red cards throughout the week to keep them fresh. My Red card today was a picture of my Dad and I walking in a crosswalk with our arms around each other in San Clemente, CA, where my parents were living at the time. My Mom took the picture, and when looking at it I can imagine her smile that day while we walked to breakfast. Sometimes when I look at this photo, it nearly brings tears to my eyes because of how much happiness it provides me. My Dad is by far the most influential person in my life when it comes to not only me as an athlete and golfer, but as a human being. He has always unconditionally been there for me.

This photo holds even more value because I almost lost my Dad in 2011. He was involved in an explosion during his time as a private contractor for the Army while stationed in Kandahar, Afghanistan. Although he still deals with some lingering issues from the explosion, thankfully he is alive and healthy! The reason I give a background for my Red card pictures is because I want to express how powerful they need to be to actually work during a moment of high stress on the golf course. They must have the power to bring you out of Red.

Thursday was a strange day. I started off very well on the front nine, shooting three under par. Steven and I were flowing very nicely, working my stories from tee box to fairway, choosing a sense from fairway to green, and really not needing my GYRA tools outside of using my GYRA scorecard. We were having fun, and I was definitely Green.

On the shuttle from #9 to #10, I stuck to the same routine of having the shuttle driver stop where we cross the street so I could walk the rest of the way. I took a glance at the wildflowers and lake behind the tee box and when it was my turn, I hit a great drive right down the middle.

I was in the middle of the fairway, 118yds out to a middle left pin. 118yds is a perfect number for my three-quarter GW. It's as if it was so perfect that I got complacent when it came to creating my moving picture. I hit such a terrible shot my level of surprise was easily a 10.

Walking up to my chip shot, I did not say a word to Steven and I most definitely did not activate any of my senses. Even worse, I did not look at my Red card that could have easily brought me out of Red and into Yellow. I would have heard the words of my Dad that I mentioned earlier "son, sometimes you just gotta be tough." I was not tough. I allowed my anger to get the best of me. Not only did I end up bogeying hole #10, I also bogeyed hole #11. I also made a very poor par on the par-five 12th. I honestly don't remember if I used any of my GYRA tools. I may have, but none of them worked because I was clearly stuck in Red.

Dr. Justice and I have known for a while now that I struggle with my anger on the course. We refer to it as The Wolf. Every single thing I do prior to a tournament and during is meant to keep The Wolf from coming out. That is why I have the GYRA tools I do. I have a clear plan to keep The Wolf at bay and I did such a poor job of it in the third round I never totally recovered. I definitely tried to use the tools to help but my subconscious was way too active.

Although I birdied #16 to get back to two under, I said to Steven, "I can't believe I am only two under, I definitely let this round get away from me." Steven responded with, "That doesn't sound like the Matty Ryan I know. Let's go, dude. Get back to being agnostic and finish tough."

The truth was I played six straight holes with my subconscious on fire and I didn't do a good enough job trying to get Green to be able to get Agnostic. I know that it is extremely important to get Green before trying to get Agnostic. If I am Red, I cannot get Agnostic. I went on to par hole #17 after hitting an excellent bunker shot to a tap-in, but

#18 was a disaster. I hit the ball in the woods to the left, punched out, missed the green, hit a pitch to 4ft, and missed the putt. I walked away from hole #18 with a double bogey and shot even par on the day. I was not happy. Very Red. I was now outside the cut line when I felt I should have been well inside it.

One of the things I had not done all year was practice after playing. The brain I just used coming off the course is not the brain that will be hitting balls on the range now. I know, neurologically, on the driving range, my brain is not able to simulate the same on-course environment it needs to address the right problem. I was exhausted, but I just felt that I needed to do a little practice. I called Dr. Justice to talk about not only round three, but the first two as well. I told him, "I think I am doing everything in my power to hit it more solid but I'm just not hitting it very well. I feel like I really, really need to practice before tomorrow's round just to feel better when I go to sleep tonight."

When I called him, I was talking insanely fast and was still Red. He knew it. He said, "Okay, Matthew, first of all, for the rest of the day, I want you to do everything very slowly. Talk slowly, walk slowly, eat slowly. You can go back to range but you need to take a couple of hours and do something for me. I want you and Steven to go off site and get some lunch."

Dr. Justice gave us an activity to do while at lunch and we would apply it to my post-round practice session. We were to write down every single thing that could go wrong during round four and every possible subconscious thought I might have. We wrote down roughly 100 different thoughts. To name a few, "Don't leave it short. Don't chunk it. Short sided again. What an idiot. Maybe I should just stop playing. What the hell am I going to do next year? Another year of hard work for nothing. I have to make this putt. I have 4 holes left and I have to play them three under." There were about 95 more and a lot of them had some choice words.

Once Steven and I finished writing out the list, we went back to the course and straight to the range. Dr. Justice wanted Steven to select a hole on the course then pick a club to hit. He would say something along the lines of, "Hole #2, you need to hit a 145yd nine iron to a back right pin with a fade that starts 3yds right of the flag and finishes 2yds left of the hole." Right before I stepped into my shot, Steven read off one of the negative thoughts on the list we made at lunch. "And remember, if you miss this pin right you are short sided and definitely won't get up and down." Or "You're probably in a divot because of how unlucky you are." We used the same technique on the putting green and chipping green. The reason Steven and I did this was to be completely prepared for all things that could happen in the fourth round, even if these thoughts came into play or not.

By rehearsing the subconscious, Dr. Justice said we were in fact activating the conscious. Many of these thoughts were already playing in my head, which is why I was talking so fast, but they were just in my head, in my subconscious. Making Steven and I bring them out actually calmed me down and made me realize what the real problem was. It was not my golf swing. It was my subconscious. It was very empowering.

That evening I was unusually calm. I FaceTimed my wife, Rachel, to tell her how the day went and how I practiced afterwards. She has been so supportive over the years and I would say she has the ability to judge my emotional temperature just seeing and hearing me over the phone. She said, "You sound great. I have all the faith in you to go get it done tomorrow. You can do it."

I knew what I needed to do. My guess was that I had to at least shoot 67 the next day to have a chance. I also received a text message from my Dad saying, "target, target, target," which I wrote in my yardage book to read the next day as my EQ focal thought. My Dad knows me so well he can look at my scorecards online and tell how I am playing.

I'm assuming he knew I wasn't hitting it great due to not making very many birdies and he knew I was putting and chipping well.

I had dinner with Bruce and Annie but skipped Jeopardy! that evening and instead watched another movie on my list, "Gladiator". After the movie I wrote down my positives and negatives for the day, did my 'better statements' and went to bed. I had a great night of sleep and the first thing I did when I woke up was watch some videos of my niece who was a year and a half old at the time. She is precious and always puts a smile on my face. I started the morning with just one goal. To be as completely Agnostic as possible doing all things. I stuck to the same morning routine but really focused on activating each sense while getting ready and making breakfast. Once again, I did change my Red card to a picture of Rachel while she was on a volunteer nursing trip in Uganda. She is holding a young boy named Oliver and they both have the biggest smiles on their faces. Although this picture is not an experience of my own, I know how much Africa means to Rachel and her smile in the picture is just incredible. It can't help but make me Green. When I stare at it, I feel like I'm there. Rachel has been such a huge part of my life while chasing my dream to play professional golf, and when I look at this picture, I feel like she is there with me every step of the way.

I stuck to my normal routine for the last day, showing up an hour and 10 minutes prior to my tee time. I was very diligent about keeping my senses activated by doing 5S before each part of my warm up. It is my firm belief that final rounds are all about EQ. They have nothing to do with mechanics. Steven was back on the bag and we were completely on the same page with how to get the job done. We have succeeded many times in the past and this year we were even more prepared, with all of the GYRA tools we have to use and learning all we have about how the brain works.

On the first tee, I was in a great place enjoying my deep micro focus. With my eyes closed I tried to listen to everything around me.

Sometimes before a round of golf, everything is so quiet you can almost hear the silence. It's hard to explain until you've experienced it yourself. I remember focusing on my breath, and when it was my turn to tee off, I opened my eyes and was ready to go. I hit driver right down the center of the fairway and we were off. As soon as we stepped off the tee box, Steven started telling me about a video my brother had sent him of Abby the night before. I received the same video and we were just dying laughing walking down the first fairway.

For the fourth round, I had Steven write down seven stories he could tell me about shared experiences we have had over the years. I thought this would be a good break from me using the stories I had used the three rounds prior. I had 120 yards to a back left pin position and hit a GW to 12ft short and left of the pin. Walking up to the green, I thought, "It would be great to get off to a good start." That is one of the thoughts I wrote on my list yesterday at lunch. Even though a positive thought, it is not Agnostic! I immediately acknowledged and replaced that thought and did a full body scan while walking to the green.

On the green, I used my moving picture to see the ball going in the hole. As I stepped in to my putt, I thought, "Make sure you get it to the hole." I had lost my picture. Not Agnostic again! I backed off of my putt and started giggling because, once again, it was another thought I had already written down the day before. Dr. Justice was right in making us write those negative thoughts because they were coming out today, and this time, I was laughing at them! I locked back into my moving picture and rolled my putt with perfect speed that fell right in the center. Hole #1 set up my whole day. I was disciplined enough to use several of my EQ tools and it paid off.

Through six holes I was three under par and was playing great. On hole #7, the long par-five, I was nearly in the same place that I was two days prior when I completely whiffed a two iron into the small pot bunker. I pulled two iron, then said to Steven, "A couple of days ago, I did not hit this very well. How do you feel about laying up?" "I've *seen you hit hundreds of good two irons. Replace that thought, focus on your picture, and knock it on the green." Steven couldn't have expressed himself any better. Not only did I hear what he said, but I looked at him and saw how confident he was in the decision to hit two iron. I hit it just on the front third of the green to a back pin. He bumped me on the shoulder as we started walking to the green and said, "All right, find ten things to see before you get up to the green."*

About 100 yards short of the green, there are two massive live oaks with Spanish moss. I literally just ran my eyes from the bottom to the top of them, engulfing myself in the beauty that surrounded me and realizing how lucky I am to play golf for a living. The pin was back middle and my back was on the front third of the green roughly 50ft away. Believe it or not, I had this same exact putt years prior and I had all of these good feelings rushing back to me. It is not an accident that my brain, when in Green, would remember a positive memory. Obviously, acknowledging and replacing, I created a great moving picture. There was never a doubt. I made the eagle putt and I was now five under through seven holes.

After a bogey on #8, I birdied number nine and made the turn at five under par for the day. Going to #10, I did some things slightly differently. I struck up a conversation with the volunteer driving the shuttle. It turned out that before moving to Florida, this man and his wife lived in my hometown of Valencia, CA, for 15 years. For the 10-minute shuttle ride, we reminisced on some of our favorite breakfast spots, and by the time I got to the tee, I was feeling very relaxed. #10 was downwind the final round and I elected to hit 3W. It had been a long time since I hit a 3W, so I pulled out my Yellow card and read about the "most gorgeous 3W I ever hit" just two weeks prior at Fazenda Boa Vista Golf Club in São Paulo, Brazil during a PGA Latino America event. I striped the ball right down the center and started telling Steven about the story on GYRA scorecard. I made a pretty steady par on #10.

On hole #11, I made a little bit of a sloppy par and I knew Steven was going to say something about it. Steven said, "Matty, you got seven holes left and I know you can do it. Be the best you have been all week in working to be Green and getting Agnostic. Let's make sure we don't leave one second for you to have a subconscious thought that you don't handle immediately. Do a quick five, dude." This is why I love Steven; he always says the right thing at the right time. Like I said before, I believe it's because he knows me extremely well. I find that to be way more valuable in a caddie than his knowledge of my game or the golf course. He made that comment for a reason and it was probably due to the fact that I looked Yellow walking off of #11.

Normally the pressure coming down the stretch at a Q-School is massive. As defined by Dr. Justice, pressure is "having too many thoughts, and most of them are negative." I did not have too many thoughts. I kept referring to what I wrote down in my yardage book the night before, "Do you have the ability to judge your current situation with no bias based on past or future?" I knew if my answer to that question was "Yes" from hole #12 to #18, I was golden.

I birdied #12 with a solid chip and a nice putt, I parred #13, bogeyed #14, and parred #15. For the first time of the day, I took a look at my Red card while walking to #16 tee. With 100% certainty I can tell you that I was not Red. My reason for looking at my Red card was because I know the nerves that start firing on the last three holes at Q-School and I planned this the night before and wrote it in my GYRA scorecard. They are impossible to ignore and I embraced them. I knew that looking at Rachel, holding Oliver, in a makeshift hospital in Uganda would definitely put things into perspective. I still had the nerves and knew they wouldn't go away, but that just means something I really care about accomplishing is within reach. Having positive thoughts about the future is not Agnostic and can be just as harmful as negative ones about the past.

As professional golfers, we always seem to have this sixth sense of where the cut line might be, whether that is qualifying for Q School or making a cut in a regular tournament. I figured I was right on the number sitting at 11 under for the week. #16 is a longer par-five, probably around 600 yards. The wind was down off the right and I was ready to launch the high ball. I could get as much wind help as possible. The last half of my moving picture came extremely easy to me on the tee. I find that wind can help create the moving picture you have a much better feel for what the last half of the flight will do.

I absolutely smoked my drive that started down the right edge of the fairway and finished right center. On the way up, I told Steven I was going to skip the story on this hole and I am going to do my own thing all the way up to the green and said, "Don't worry," with a smile. I wrote in my GYRA scorecard "behind closed doors." This refers to a song titled Behind Closed Doors by one of my favorite bands, Rise Against. The message in the song that stands out to me is that there is no quit when you're fighting for something you believe in. Walking to my second shot, I took an ACT breath, and as I released it, I actually recited the lyrics to the song all while hearing my breathing and each word.

For the second shot, I had 265 yards to a back left pin that is extremely hard to get close to even with a wedge. My plan was to hit a two iron that finished just right of the green knowing that a chip and a putt was my best chance to make birdie. I did 10-2 with my grip and hit a great two iron that went exactly where I was hoping it would go. Immediately after my shot, I gave myself three positives. "I have a great short game. I got my best friend on the bag. What beautiful scenery." After that, I continued with my breathing and completely relaxed my upper body all the way up to the green, attempting to get my shoulders and jaw as tension free as possible. I pitched a 58-degree wedge up to 6 feet for birdie. This putt was breaking left to right and nearly a full cup. I used my moving picture to get completely Agnostic over the ball and could literally feel the speed of the ball rolling into the cup. I made it for birdie.

After nearly making birdie on the par-three #17, I walked up the hill to #18 tee where I made double bogey the day before. I read about a drive I had written down on my Yellow card and got very specific with my target. My drive ended up slightly in the rough down the left side of the hole. I went into story mode, telling Steven about another great friend of mine who I have known my entire life. It was a story about my friend Sean Norton who I grew up playing football with at the age of five all the way through high school. Our Dads have been best friends since they were five and are still best friends to this day. Sean played football at Fresno State University, where I played golf, and we were roommates for a couple years.

The story in my GYRA Scorecard is about the first time Sean ran onto the field for a college game. He ran on the field to replace the starting quarterback who went out with an injury. Sean was a very highly touted player coming out of high school and everyone at Fresno State had been dying to see him play. I still get chills telling this story. Not only did Sean get his shot, he performed like a champion. The first play, he threw a 10-yard out route to a receiver on the right sideline. The second play of the drive, he ran the ball for another first down and stepped out of bounds. The third play, he threw a deep ball in the back-right corner of the end zone for a touchdown to future NFL tight end Bear Pascoe. I get so fully immersed in this story I can't help but give my mind a rest and feel Green.

My second shot on #18, I hit a six iron that just got absolutely swallowed by the wind blowing off of the right. I missed the green short and left to a front left pin. I was short sided again, another potential surprise that I wrote down at lunch the day before but again, a smile on my face recognizing that negative thought. My sense walking up to the green was to relax the lower body as much as I could and I also pulled out my Yellow card. I had replaced my "pitch" shot on my Yellow card after the second round and wrote down a couple of the pitches I hit that day. These Yellow card shots I was reading were extremely fresh and made it very easy to recall the shots and rekindle those good feelings of pulling it off when it really counted. I set my moving picture and held onto it until I hit my shot. I hit a great high lofted pitch to one foot, and then went up and tapped it in.

I finished the day with one eagle, six birdies, and two bogeys, shooting a six under 66. Steven and I gave each other a big high five and a huge hug. We knew I had qualified. When the tournament was all said and done, I ended up finishing 10th at 12 under par. There were 19 qualifying spots and the number fell at 10 under par. Every shot mattered in the last round. All of the EQ work I had put in throughout the week culminated in a near flawless final round. By front loading my week with emotionally uplifting activities and having faith in executing my EQ diet, I was able to enter the last day with a clear gameplay, tons of stored energy, and clear picture on exactly how to get the job done.

There is no reason any one of you cannot learn this, and repeat it over and over again, giving yourself chances to play in your zone.

I hope that this book has been a journey of learning for you, one that takes the wonderful sport of golf and brings out the best in you. Training to be your best for your important round is the same as training to be your best in life. Now, what could be better?

To learn more, go to www.gyragolf.com

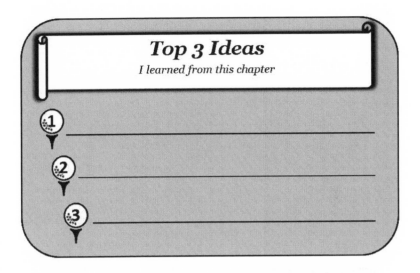

Top 3 Ideas
I learned from this chapter

1 _____

2 _____

3 _____

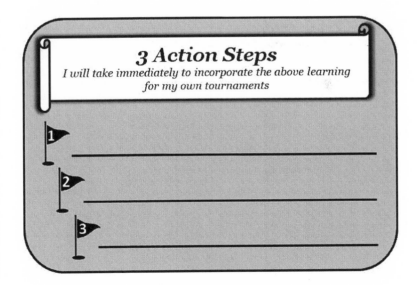

3 Action Steps
I will take immediately to incorporate the above learning for my own tournaments

1 _____

2 _____

3 _____